FILM
SCRIPTS

LE PETIT SOLDAT
a film by
Jean-Luc Godard

English translation and description of action
by Nicholas Garnham

Simon and Schuster, New York

Published by Simon and Schuster
Rockefeller Center, 630 Fifth Avenue
New York, New York 10020
First printing

General Editor: Sandra Wake

Stills by courtesy of the Academy Cinema
and *Cahiers du Cinéma*

SBN 671-20682-6
Library of Congress Catalog Card Number: 72-119355

Manufactured in Great Britain by Villiers Publications Ltd,
London NW5

CONTENTS

SHOOTING *LE PETIT SOLDAT*

'. . . The subject of *Le Petit Soldat* is not a contemporary subject but a news subject, using in other words a camera held in the hand (like the clenched fist of the Spanish republicans in *L'Espoir*), quite a few whip-pans, over- and under-exposed shots, one or two blurred ones, to tell the story of a French secret agent who refuses to carry out a mission, but ends up by doing so, after one or two misadventures, including his arrest and torture by an enemy organisation. In fact, this story for the benefit of the distributors, once deciphered, becomes that of a man who finds that the face he sees in a mirror does not correspond to the idea he has of what lies behind it, a man who thinks that women should be older than twenty-five, a man who likes the music of good old Joseph Haydn, a man who would like to be able to cut his way through with a dagger like the others, a man who is very proud of being French, because he likes Joachim du Bellay and Louis Aragon, and really he's still only a little boy, which is why I called him *Le Petit Soldat*.' Jean-Luc Godard (*Cahiers du Cinéma*, no. 109, July, 1960).

[In *Le Petit Soldat*] I wanted to achieve the realism, the concreteness that I had missed in *A Bout de Souffle*. The film is based on an idea I had had for a long time : I wanted to say something about brainwashing. A prisoner was told: 'It may take twenty minutes or twenty years, but someone can always be made to talk.' As a result of the events in Algeria I replaced brainwashing by torture, which had become a burning topic. My prisoner is someone who is asked to do something and does not want to do it. He just doesn't want to, and he digs in his heels, as a matter of principle. That is liberty as I see it — from a practical point of view. To be free is to be able to do what one pleases and when one pleases.

The film should have something to say about its period. People talk about politics in it, but it is not politically orientated in a particular direction. The way I approached it was to say to myself: people complain that the Nouvelle Vague only shows people in bed, I'm going to show some who are in politics and don't have time to go to bed with each other. Now politics meant Algeria. But I had to show it from the aspect that I knew and in the way I felt it. If Kyrou or the people on *L'Observateur* wanted it represented differently, fine — they would just have to go to the F.L.N. in Tripoli or elsewhere with a camera. If Dupont wanted another point of view he had only to film Algeria from the point of view of the paras. It hasn't been done and that is a pity. Personally I was speaking about things which concerned me in 1960 as a Parisian belonging to no political party. The thing which I was concerned with was the problem of war and its moral repercussions. So I showed a character who sets himself all kinds of problems. He doesn't know how to resolve them, but to formulate them even in a confused way is already to try and resolve them. It is perhaps better to ask oneself some questions rather than to refuse to face any problems, or to believe oneself capable of resolving everything.

JEAN-LUC GODARD, 1960

9

INTERVIEW WITH JEAN-LUC GODARD

by Yvonne Baby

GODARD : It is the story of a French refugee in Switzerland who belongs to a counter-terrorist group and who is asked to kill a man. He doesn't want to but he ends up by accepting.

BABY : *He is also taken prisoner and tortured by F.L.N. agents. Why?*

GODARD : I feel that I can say something about torture, paradoxically, because I have not been subjected to it. In any case I say very little about it, or rather I deal with it in a very detached manner. I dislike appealing to people's pity and I find it indecent to 'glorify pain.' I have often wondered if, under torture, I would be able to keep my mouth shut. I don't know, but I wanted to tackle this subject.

BABY : *The little soldier does keep his mouth shut.*

GODARD : Yes, but as he has no cause to defend he's not being particularly heroic. And then it's natural to try and resist as much as possible. It's a reaction which makes one glimpse and understand other things, but that is already the subject of another film. I also wanted to show that one can torture someone from political motives, and not only to get addresses or telephone numbers out of him. In the film I quote a phrase of Napoleon's which can also be applied to our age : 'Today tragedy is politics.'

BABY : *In what way is your film political?*

GODARD : It is political insofar as the action is politically motivated, in the same way as one can consider Balzac's *Une Ténébreuse Affaire* as a political novel, in contrast, for example, to *La Cousine Bette.* But one can say that the film is not a political one because I do not take sides and the sub-

10

ject is not 'slanted' in the manner of Russian films.

The little soldier himself loves a girl who works for the F.L.N. I would like people to understand the attitude of the French and the others, and that's why I showed a girl who was in the opposing camp. It is a film which will no doubt displease those on the right and those on the left equally. Personally, I don't take sides: I'm for the little soldier and the girl at the same time. I have told the story of an agent of the right, but I could just as well do a film on the life of Djamilla Bouhired.

In any case, the little soldier is both right wing and left wing, because he is a sentimentalist. He is — in a classical film — a romantic character who reasons in a leftist manner in a rightist situation: he is close to both Drieu la Rochelle's Gilles and Louis Aragon's Aurélien at the same time. If he had to choose, he would no doubt be on the other side. He hankers after a more revolutionary past. He says: 'Around 1930, young people had a revolution . . . They had the Spanish Civil War . . . We have nothing.' Today, we live in a less lyrical period. One is more compelled to find truth inside oneself rather than outside. The little soldier is searching for truth, he is searching for what is most important: that is to say not to be defeated, not to be bitter, to continue being active, to feel free. But even when everything is going wrong he feels that he should not have any regrets. He says: 'I had lost my freedom.' And again: 'For me, the time for action is over — I have aged. The time for reflection begins.'

I have made an adventure film, but it remains an individualistic one; *Le Petit Soldat* is a sort of essay on the behaviour of a secret agent which deals with the problems of an individual. If one wants to deal with generalities, then one writes books of philosophy or goes into politics, but that is not the case with me.

BABY : *Do you feel close to your character?*

11

GODARD : I find it easy to identify myself with him. Although none of the things which happen in the film have happened to me, I can imagine myself as a deserter, or this slightly naïve adventurer who resembles the students in Nizan's *La Conspiration*, and who finally allows himself to be dragged into this affair. I thought it out in relation to myself, and my own character is close to that of Michel Subor, who plays the part of the little soldier. Also Subor resembles his character just as Belmondo resembled his in *A Bout de Souffle*. What I really show is a man who analyses himself and discovers that he is different from the concept he had of himself. Personally, when I look at myself in a mirror I have the same feeling.

I have been influenced by Malraux and particularly by *Les Noyers de l'Altenburg*. But in the cinema it is very difficult to introduce philosophical discussions, so one can only show an action which will lead the spectators to ask themselves questions about this action. While working on the film I felt that I had to get somewhere and I have the impression that I was groping towards something, but what? — something that was beautiful and important. In effect, the film is a series of questions as to what is beautiful and important.

Of course, it would have been better if it had been thought out over five or six years, but I'm lazy, and I was activated by contemporary events. In order to find subjects, one only needs to look at what is going on around us. A film must be of its period. The cloche hat is less interesting today than it was in 1925, and it is quite right that *Quai des Brumes* should appear dated. I would be incapable of making a film about the Resistance. People then had a way of talking and feeling which bears no relation to the way we behave today.

1960

INTRODUCTION

' For me, the time for action is over. I have aged. The time for reflection begins.' These, the opening words of *Le Petit Soldat,* Godard's second full-length film, describe not only the state of mind of Bruno Forestier but also of Jean-Luc Godard. His first feature film *A Bout de Souffle* was an instinctive film, very much a gesture, a gamble. It was also an immense, world-wide, critical and commercial success. For Godard things could never be as straightforward again. He would now be judged differently and inevitably must judge himself differently. And so with his next film *Le Petit Soldat* he started that alternating rhythm that has run right through his work, films of action and instinct, *Une Femme est une Femme,* or *Bande à Part,* alternating with very personal meditations, *Vivre Sa Vie* or *Pierrot Le Fou.*

So *Le Petit Soldat* is a film of reflection. Bruno Forestier is in a sense meditating upon the life and actions of Michel Poiccard, the hero of *A Bout de Souffle.* Michel never thought about what he did. He represented in a very pure and simple form the post-war generation, in rebellion against all the received opinions and standards of that previous generation which caused and fought the Second World War. But he did not know why he rebelled. He hardly knew he was rebelling. Bruno, on the other hand, is much closer to Godard himself. He is blessed or perhaps he is cursed by self-consciousness and intelligence. He may not know why he rebels, but he wants to find out. In fact, this quest is the motivating power of the film. As Bruno himself says, ' Perhaps after all asking questions is more important than finding answers.'

At what problems do Bruno — and through him Godard — direct their questions?

Godard has said, ' Film is like a personal diary, a note-book or a monologue by someone who tries to justify himself before a camera that is almost an accuser, like one does before a lawyer or a psychiatrist.' In *Le Petit Soldat,* Godard through Bruno Forestier is trying to justify his very reason for living. The film is an enquiry into the nature of indi-viduality. It asks the question, ' Who am I ? '

Godard first takes one of the central tenets of French philosophy, Descartes's celebrated dictum, ' I think, therefore I am.' But in Godard's world, which is our world, the prop of thought has been destroyed by psychological research. Bruno, by constantly talking, tries to trap his thoughts on the wing. As he puts it, ' Perhaps people talk without stopping like gold prospectors . . . to find the truth. Instead of panning the bottom of the river, they pan the bottom of their own thoughts.' But his thoughts move too fast to be caught. So too do other people's. Bruno is constantly asking Veronica what she is thinking. Often she just doesn't know. Bruno at one point remarks : ' What's important is not the way others see you, it's the way you see yourself.' But Godard shows in the film that in this as in so much else Bruno is wrong. The quest for individuality leads to disaster, to murder and death, which after all are the opposite of individuality, but it doesn't lead Bruno to a clearer picture of who he is. The excessive indi-vidualism of Michel Poiccard is shown to be no answer.

In *Vivre Sa Vie,* Nana says, ' I may forget that I am responsible, but I am, all the same.' This sense of inescapable responsibility, of no man being an island, as an alternative to individualism, first enters Godard's work with *Le Petit Soldat.* And in its train comes politics, one of the forms that mutual responsibility takes in our society. Politics first joins Godard's world with *Le Petit Soldat.* It will never leave it. Indeed to date, Godard remains the most political of film-makers. This

14

is ironical when so many people regard Godard as the apostle of uncaring anarchism. When the New Wave started, many people accused its directors of avoiding important subjects. *A Bout de Souffle* was seen by these people as final confirmation that these young film makers were interested only in crime and young people jumping in and out of bed. So it came as something of a shock when *Le Petit Soldat* was banned. But the ban, in a sense, established Godard's political credentials. Whatever anyone else subsequently thought of this story of Arab-French counter-terrorism, the French authorities took it seriously enough to ban it. But, like the hero of *Masculin-Féminin* and the heroine of *Made in USA,* Bruno cannot find a place for himself in politics. He desperately wants to be idealistic, but he cannot be. And so he both resists torture and kills, for personal not political reasons and without conviction. In this film, as in *Made in USA,* politics has become a strange, violent and apparently meaningless game. Both Right and Left have become indistinguishable in their methods. Both Laszlo of the FLN and Jacques, his right wing opponent, use exactly the same phrase to Bruno. ' You must sometimes have the strength to cut a way through with a dagger.' But this dangerous game seems to have less and less to do with the thoughts and feelings of ordinary people. Hence Bruno's nostalgia for the more innocent, simple days of the 1930s and the Spanish Civil War. So politics, too, fails to answer Bruno's questions.

Yet perhaps love, another form of mutual responsibility, defines personality. Perhaps Bruno can find a meaning for his life in his relationship with Veronica. But this way ends in Bruno's betrayal and Veronica's death. Nonetheless, love retains a particular value for Godard, because it is an escape from thought, almost a negation of thought. In Godard's films, love is an act of faith that one makes in spite of oneself. In the Bible thought came into the Garden of Eden and destroyed love. Godard tries to reverse this process. Whatever

15

its weakness, love for Godard is man's only hope of salvation. The desperation of Godard's films lies in the terrifying flimsiness of this one hope. It is something that we can't choose. When Bruno is first told by Hugh about Veronica, he doesn't want to meet her, and says that girls are just a bloody nuisance. In fact the more we see of Veronica during the film, the more we disagree with Bruno's opinion. And yet Bruno acknowledges that he has undergone something akin to a conversion when he pays Hugh the fifty dollars he bet that he wouldn't fall in love with her. He is powerless to control it. But because love can't be controlled and because it requires reciprocation from another who is likewise out of control, it is an inherently fragile sentiment. Bruno is always asking Veronica if she loves him, and we never really know whether she does or not. Later in *Le Mépris* Paul will destroy the love his wife has for him by continually questioning her. As we can never be sure that our love is reciprocated, love makes us lonelier than ever, more aware of the impossibility of knowing who we or anyone else really is.

Veronica, the object of this love, is played by Anna Karina. It was the first time Godard used her in his films. He married her shortly afterwards. In *Le Petit Soldat* Godard's camera, like Bruno with his camera, tries to trap Karina, tries to discover who she is, what she is thinking. This probing is part of Godard's questioning method. But it is painful both to him the director and to us the spectators. To us, because of an uncertainty as to what will happen next, and because of an unwished intimacy. To the director, because he is frightened of the cruelty of his own medium. In this film, as in later Godard films, we are never sure whether we are watching Karina acting or just being. For Godard the two are inextricably confused. In a Godard film, characters act out their lives in order to discover who they are. This is the significance in the film of the quotation from Cocteau's *Thomas L'Imposteur,* ' William flew, leapt, ran like

16

a hare. Without hearing the shots, he stopped and turned round out of breath. Then he felt a terrible blow on his chest. He fell, he became deaf and blind. A bullet, he said to himself. I'm finished unless I pretend to be dead . . . but with him, fiction and reality were one, William Thomas was dead.' The director tracks these characters like a big-game hunter. The camera and the gun are the two objects most closely associated with Bruno. Bruno's questioning of Veronica is mirrored in the film by the FLN torturing Bruno. Bruno tortures Veronica with his questions and his camera. Godard tortures his actors with his camera.

It is this anguish before the documentary nature of his medium that leads Godard in later films increasingly to break up the flow of his films in order to make them as artificial as possible with captions, songs, etc. But in *Le Petit Soldat* we see this beautiful cruelty, this probing in its pure state, in this first confrontation between Godard and Karina. But already, Godard, like Bruno, in Wilde's phrase, can see himself destroying the thing he loves. But he cannot stop, for he, like Bruno, is in love. He is in love with the cinema. And the cinema, as Bruno says, ' is the truth twenty-four times a second.' Godard himself has said, ' If the modern novel is fear of the blank page, modern painting is fear of the blank canvas . . . why shouldn't modern cinema be fear of the camera, fear of the dialogue, fear of the actors, fear of montage?'

Nicholas Garnham

CREDITS :

Written and directed by	Jean-Luc Godard
Assistant to the director	Francis Cognany
Director of Photography	Raoul Coutard
Camera Operator	Michel Latouche
Editor	Agnès Guillemot
Script-girl	Suzanne Schiffman
Assistants to the editor	Nadine Marquand, Lili Herman
Music	Maurice Leroux
Sound	Jacques Maumont
Producer	Georges de Beauregard
Production company	de Beauregard/Société Nouvelle de Cinéma
Process	Black and White
Running time	88 mins
Made on Location in	Geneva, April-May 1960

Banned by the French Censor Board and Minister of Information; passed with minor cuts and first shown in 1963.

CAST :

Bruno Forestier	Michel Subor
Véronica Dreyer	Anna Karina
Jacques	Henri-Jacques Huet
Paul	Paul Beauvais
Laszlo	Laszlo Szabo
Beauregard	Georges de Beauregard
Bystander at railway station	Jean-Luc Godard

LE PETIT SOLDAT

The half light of dawn. In the middle distance a lone man in an open Chevrolet stops at a frontier post. As the frontier guard examines his papers, he lights a cigarette.

BRUNO *off :* For me, the time for action is over — I have aged. The time for reflection begins.

The car pulls away from the frontier and disappears into the gloom.

Daylight. Over BRUNO'S *shoulder, as he drives, we see the streets of Geneva. The camera pans to the right and shows the lake. The car is crossing a bridge.*

BRUNO *off :* Geneva. Its rather pretty lake, the Léman, cuts the town in two. Three days ago the secret agents of several countries openly took part, here on neutral territory, in a fight to the death.

Interior of a bank. BRUNO'S *car pulls up outside. He jumps out without opening the door and runs into the bank. The camera follows him as, stuffing a cigarette into his mouth, he approaches the counter.*

BRUNO : Eight hundred dollars.

As BRUNO *waits for his money he lights a cigarette.*

BRUNO *off :* Suddenly I thought of myself : Bruno Forestier, a reporter for the French News Agency, looking for anything important round here.

The cashier counts out his money.

Close up : Newspaper placard. MORE TERRORIST ATTACKS. BRUNO *buys a paper and, leafing through it, walks along the street and gets into his car.*

19

Close up : Headlines in the paper. Tilt down to a photograph of the assassination. He mutters to himself.

BRUNO : They're at it again! Damn and blast! They're completely crazy!

As BRUNO *drives along in his Chevrolet the camera pans from the buildings and streets of a sunlit Geneva to* BRUNO *and back again.*

BRUNO *off :* Geneva 13th May 1958. What were those lines of Aragon? ' But who was not unhappy with June stabbed.'

BRUNO *pulls up at the kerb and, snatching a camera from the back seat, begins taking photographs. He is photographing a young couple kissing beside a poster which reads LOVE ONE ANOTHER. The couple turn to look at* BRUNO. *He puts away his camera and drives off.* BRUNO *leaps out of his car and rushes into an office building, unloading his camera as he goes and tossing the cassette in the air.*

From behind a closed door on which there is a notice FRENCH NEWS AGENCY we hear BRUNO *ask.*

BRUNO : How's things, Mary Lou?

MARY LOU : Someone just rang for you, Mr Forestier.

BRUNO *angry and petulant :* You said I was here . . . But why Mary Lou, you are a bloody nuisance. I told you not to say I was in.

A quick shot of BRUNO *driving.*

Dusk. Street lights and car head lamps glimmer. BRUNO'S *car passes and disappears over the bridge across a lake ringed by neon lights.*

BRUNO *off :* The dark blue of the sky reminded me of a picture by Paul Klee. ' Where have you come from? Where are you? Where are you going? Do dove, dove, verso dove.'

Daylight. Close up : BRUNO'S *hands hold a postcard of a Paul Klee painting. He stands by a newspaper kiosk examining it. From off someone shouts.*

HUGH *off :* Well, man, what's up?

20

Bruno *walks round the kiosk and shakes hands with* Hugh *who is sitting at a café table.*

Hugh : Good-bye, Bruno, what are you doing here?

Bruno *hands him the postcard.*

Bruno : It's beautiful this Klee.

Hugh : Not as beautiful as the girl I've got a date with.

Bruno *has wandered back to the kiosk.*

Bruno : What girl? *He shouts.*

Hugh : I told her you'd take some photographs of her, come on.

Bruno : What am I getting mixed up in, and supposing I don't want to see her?

Bruno *rejoins* Hugh *and they walk off still talking.*

Hugh : Supposing, supposing, come on, come on.

Bruno : I must go via the Brazilian Consulate.

Hugh : No, no, you can go tomorrow.

Still walking Bruno *lights a cigarette.*

Bruno : No, it's a bloody nuisance, with girls, you are always messed around . . . Is it the Danish girl who was with Michael yesterday?

Hugh : Good, so you know her?

Continuing their conversation, they go down some steps and disappear into the crowd.

Bruno : No, but he told me about her, as I was coming out of the 58 Club.

Hugh : I bet you'll want to sleep with her . . . She's got a mouth like Leslie Caron.

Bruno : No. I only sleep with girls I'm in love with.

Hugh : Well, in that case, I bet that in five minutes you'll be in love with her.

Bruno : How much do you bet? 50 dollars?

Hugh : If you want.

Bruno : 50 dollars I don't fall in love with her.

They drive through the busy street of Geneva in Bruno's *Chevrolet.* Hugh *turns and waves to someone.*

25

BRUNO *off :* The first time I met Veronica, she looked as if she had come straight out of a play by Jean Giraudoux.

> VERONICA *is standing on the pavement talking to a man who gives her a little toy dog. They shake hands and part.* VERONICA *walks off gaily swinging her arms towards the Chevrolet. She gets in between* BRUNO *and* HUGH *and as they drive off into the traffic the camera pans up to the statue of a general on horseback. From the back seat the camera peers over the shoulders of* BRUNO, VERONICA *and* HUGH *as they drive through the streets of Geneva. As they talk the camera pans from side to side to show sometimes* HUGH *and* VERONICA, *sometimes* BRUNO *and* VERONICA. HUGH *fingers* VERONICA'S *hair.*

HUGH : Kill a fellow in the back, okay . . . but with a revolver at least, or a knife, but not with a bomb.

> *He puts his arm round* VERONICA'S *shoulder.*

HUGH : It's true, killing a man from a distance, I think it's dishonest.

BRUNO : You don't know anything about it.

> VERONICA *looks at herself in a mirror, re-arranging her hair.*

VERONICA : What are you talking about?

> *The camera pans back and forth.*

VERONICA : What are you talking about?

HUGH : Lachenal, the History of Art Professor who was killed yesterday. They put a bomb in his car.

VERONICA : Who?

BRUNO *to* HUGH : What do you know about it? You don't even know what you're talking about. It gets on my nerves. Students, they're all the same.

> BRUNO *and* VERONICA *look at one another.*

VERONICA : I knew his daughter. She often came to the skating rink. You're right, it's awful.

> *Suddenly, as they are driving along, a leather jacketed*

26

photographer takes a photograph of them.
Close up : BRUNO *looking angry.*
The photographer rushes up gesturing them to stop. As the car stops he takes another photograph and shoves a card into BRUNO'S *hand.*
Close up : BRUNO *unfolds the card. It is a street photographer's order card with a number and address on it. They drive off.*

BRUNO : Damn and blast!

HUGH : What's up, man?

BRUNO : I must go to the station.

BRUNO *off* : They thought I said : to the war.* So, I told them it was the same thing. Again, she stared at me.

A view of Geneva from high above the bridge over the lake. BRUNO *gets out of his car.*

BRUNO : Right, I must be off.

He walks round the car and joins VERONICA *and* HUGH.

BRUNO : For the photographs, tomorrow at five.

HUGH : But where are you going?

BRUNO : Mystery.

HUGH : You, you really are mysterious.

BRUNO : Yes, I'm a secret agent.

BRUNO *lights a cigarette, leaves them and crosses the road, he turns back to wave.*
Close up : VERONICA *looking after him, she is smoking.* BRUNO *hesitates and runs back across the road after* HUGH *and* VERONICA, *who are walking away. He taps* VERONICA *on the shoulder. She turns.*

BRUNO : Do that with your hair.

BRUNO *shakes his head back and forth.*
Close up : VERONICA *imitates him, her hair swirling round her head.* BRUNO *takes out some money.* VERONICA *looks from one to the other mystified.*

---

* Translation note : This pun depends on the French words gare/ station and guerre/war sounding the same.

BRUNO : There's fifty dollars.

BRUNO *hands the money to* HUGH *and leaves them.* HUGH *calls after him.*

HUGH : But, where are you off to? Just a moment, it's important.

BRUNO *turns :* You never know what is important.

HUGH *and* VERONICA *walk away, occasionally looking back at* BRUNO.

BRUNO *off :* I was still very stupid and very young.

BRUNO, *wearing dark glasses, rushes into the station pushing people out of his way.*

BRUNO *off :* Would it be fine? Would it rain? Impossible to say.

BRUNO *stops, takes off his dark glasses, looks at the street photographer's card which he has taken from his pocket and looks up.*

Close up : Train Timetable. The camera pans down the times. 13.23, 13.37. It stops at 16.00 and then returns to 14.18.

Close up : BRUNO.

Close up : Photographer's ticket No. 1418.

Close up : BRUNO.

Close up : Train timetable.

Pan right to show destination Wym-Lausanne.

BRUNO *sits in a moving train. Shots of* BRUNO *are intercut with those of fellow passengers and the passing countryside.* BRUNO *is waiting for something to happen, but it is a normal boring train journey.*

BRUNO *off :* Up to now my story has been simple. It's about a fellow without ideals. And tomorrow?

BRUNO *leans over and asks a fellow passenger wearing dark glasses for a light. The man makes no reply.*

BRUNO *off :* I asked if he had a light.

The journey continues. BRUNO *is restless and bored. He examines his fellow passengers. The two men opposite*

*are carrying on a long complicated animated conver-
sation, which we cannot hear properly. We share
Bruno's frustration. Once more Bruno leans across and
asks the same man for a light. Again the man does not
reply.*

Bruno *off :* I asked again if perhaps he had a light.

Bruno *off :* Sometimes I get the impression of having wasted
my time.

*The journey continues. They pass a station called
GLAND. A few minutes later Bruno gets up and leaves
the carriage. The man in dark glasses watches him go.
The camera pans to a young woman with a child.*

Bruno *off :* And Veronica, are her eyes Velasquez grey or
Renoir grey?

*The camera pans back to the man in dark glasses who
signals to someone outside the window. A man stands
waiting by a Citroen.*

Bruno *off :* Usually it's Alfred Latouche or his young brother
Etienne who comes for me. But they ended up getting themselves pinched.

Bruno *stands in the middle of the road, smoking.*

Bruno *off :* And me?

*He throws away his cigarette and buttoning up his
jacket, walks off.*

*A Citroen turns into a tree-lined drive. As it passes the
front of the house, a shirt-sleeved man leans out of the
window and then shoves a gun into his belt. Bruno gets
out of the Citroen. It drives off and he walks towards
the house looking up at some men on a balcony over
the front door.*

*Paul and Jacques come out of the house pulling on
their jackets and opening the door of a white Peugeot,
they gesture Bruno into the back seat.*

Radio Message *over : Then there were clashes with the CRS*

who used tear-gas grenades . . . around five o'clock the para-
chutists joined in . . . that is the latest information we have
received.

PAUL : Go on, get in.
  The Peugeot drives off and stops as it reaches the road-
  way.
BRUNO *off :* The anti-terrorist commando, of which I was
part, was financed by an ex-Poujadist deputy, who, once upon
a time, had had his moment of glory with Vichy.
  As we hear BRUNO's *voice we see a large American car*
  parked across the road. A chauffeur opens the back door
  and two men, LOBJEOIS *and* BEAUREGARD, *get out.*
  JACQUES *goes over and shakes* LOBJEOIS' *hand.*
LOBJEOIS *to* BEAUREGARD : You know Jacques?
BEAUREGARD *nods towards* BRUNO.
BEAUREGARD : It's him?
  BRUNO *and* PAUL *are sitting in the Peugeot looking across*
  at the others.

RADIO MESSAGE *over*: *André Migou, our lobby correspondent,*
10 pm, Mr Pflimlin has asked . . . the government has asked
for the break up of certain subversive organisations.

BRUNO *off :* I didn't know the other one.
BEAUREGARD : . . . the guy you told me about.
LOBJEOIS : No, no, there he is, in the back of the Peugeot.
  BRUNO *turns to* PAUL.
BRUNO : Who is he?
PAUL : If anyone asks, say you don't know.
  BEAUREGARD *gives* JACQUES *some money.* JACQUES *shakes*
  hands and walks back to the Peugeot. BEAUREGARD
  waves, shouts ' Good luck', and gets into his car with
  LOBJEOIS. JACQUES *gets into the Peugeot.*

BRUNO *off* : Go-betweens, bankers, car salesmen, parachutists, poor little rich boys . . . the secret war shook men and ideas in a rhythm which became more bloody every day.

The Peugeot and the large American car drive off in opposite directions.

Inside the Peugeot PAUL *drives, while* JACQUES *sits in the back with* BRUNO. *As they drive along, the camera cuts and pans between them, following the flow of their conversation.*

JACQUES : Are we early, or not?

PAUL : It's okay, ten to five.

JACQUES : Good. If his car is there, stop near the fountain, Popaul, where I showed you yesterday. You'll see it, a 57 Nash convertible. Well, little Bruno . . . ?

BRUNO, *a cigarette in his mouth, replies with a surly* . . .

BRUNO : What?

JACQUES : What are you thinking?

BRUNO : I don't know.

JACQUES : You must know, Bruno. What were you going to say?

BRUNO : Nothing.

JACQUES : But you were. Look here, snap out of it.

BRUNO : Yes, but I've changed my mind.

JACQUES *takes a book out of his pocket.*

BRUNO : What's that book?

JACQUES : ' Thomas The Imposter.'

BRUNO : Oh yes, Jean Cocteau.

JACQUES : Listen to the end, it's great.

He begins to read.

JACQUES *reading :* ' William flew, leapt, ran like a hare. Without hearing the shots, he stopped, and turned round out of breath.'

BRUNO *throws his cigarette out of the window. They are driving along featureless country roads.*

JACQUES *continues his reading.*

31

JACQUES *reading :* ' Then he felt a terrible blow on his chest. He fell, he became deaf and blind. A bullet, he said to himself. I'm finished unless I pretend to be dead . . .'

Close up : BRUNO.

JACQUES *reading :* ' . . . but with him, fiction and reality were one, William Thomas was dead.'

JACQUES *closes the book and looks at* BRUNO.

JACQUES : It's beautiful.

BRUNO *looks at* JACQUES *defiantly, an unlit cigarette in his mouth.*

BRUNO : Yes, I'd like to die like that.

PAUL : Perhaps you will, before very long.

BRUNO : What's the matter with you? Why?

BRUNO *lights his cigarette.*

JACQUES : Because you're a bloody nuisance, my old friend. We've been looking for you since Saturday. What did you go to Annecy for?

BRUNO *off :* If only Veronica could come with me to Brazil; that would be ideal.

BRUNO : I'm setting up an art gallery. I went to buy three small Modiglianis.

JACQUES : Luckily I'm not asking you what you're using for money.

BRUNO : Okay, okay, I'll give it back to you. I'll sell them for seven million in Geneva.

PAUL : Here we are.

They approach a small radio-station.

BRUNO *off :* ' O month of bloom, month of metamorphosis. I will never forget the lilacs or the roses.' Why was I obsessed by that poem?

RADIO MESSAGE *over :* . . . *the Algerian war is a war imposed on a people* . . .

JACQUES : Turn down the radio.

Close up : A hand turns the knob of the car radio.
The Peugeot is parked at the side of the road. In the
back sit BRUNO *and* JACQUES; *in front* PAUL, *he is looking*
at his watch.

JACQUES : Do you know the guy doing that broadcast?
BRUNO : Isn't it Arthur Palivoda of Radio Geneva?
JACQUES : Yes, that's right.
PAUL : There he is!

In the driveway of the radio-station, watched by the
trio in the Peugeot, PALIVODA *gets into an open Nash*
convertible.

BRUNO *off :* I quickly guessed what it was all about. They
suspected me of being a double agent.

As PALIVODA *drives off, the camera pans to the Peugeot.*
JACQUES : Okay, let's go.
RADIO MESSAGE *over :* . . . *a war between Europeans and*
Arabs, not between Moslems and Christians, you are at this
very moment dying of that very illusion . . .

The camera pans back to show PALIVODA *driving off,*
followed by the Peugeot.
Close up : A hand retunes the car radio.
From inside the Peugeot we see PALIVODA'S *Nash driving*
ahead down yet another nondescript country road. In
the background we hear a voice on the radio.

PAUL : Fancy that programme being called 'A Neutral
Speaks.' It breaks me up.
JACQUES : You've seen Palivoda before?
BRUNO : Before today? No.
JACQUES *to* BRUNO : Popaul will drive up alongside him. Take
a good look. Because you're going to have to kill him.
BRUNO : Why me again?
JACQUES : I received the order from Paris. I'm just passing
it on.

As they talk PAUL *draws alongside* PALIVODA. BRUNO

33

and JACQUES *both look at him.*

BRUNO *off* : Jacques told me it was very easy.

JACQUES : All you've got to do is drive up alongside him, like Paul's doing now, and fire when you're level with him.

PALIVODA looks across at them.

JACQUES : Wind the window up, damn it!

The Peugeot draws ahead. BRUNO *turns and looks at the disappearing Nash through the back window.*

BRUNO : They're sure, in Paris, he's working for the rebels? That surprises me for a Swiss.

PAUL : Not me — it's less dangerous to talk on the radio than fight. The Swiss have never been brave, you've just got to watch them drive. They put out their indicator to pass a cyclist. That makes me livid. Shall I go by the hotel?

JACQUES : No. We'll go there later. Go to the office!

BRUNO : Is it true that Latouche is dead?

JACQUES : Yes. They found him on Tuesday in the bathroom of his room at the Bristol Hotel. They'd cut out his tongue and ripped off his eyelids. There was blood everywhere. Are you frightened, then?

BRUNO : Do you think it amuses me to shoot people?

PAUL : We'll lend you the Peugeot if you want. It hasn't got a Geneva number plate. You'll be less conspicuous with it.

BRUNO : It's too dangerous. Why me, not Paul?

JACQUES leans forward and lights his cigarette from PAUL's lighter.

JACQUES : Because you . . .

BRUNO : No, Jacques, it bothers me, killing Palivoda.

JACQUES : What's the matter with you?

BRUNO : It's funny, nothing now, but three seconds ago, yes. Why? I don't know. Suddenly I feel that if I was to shoot Palivoda, it would be a defeat.

JACQUES : That doesn't matter.

BRUNO : It does. Victory is better than defeat.

Bruno *holds his clenched fist up beside his head, palm forward.*

Bruno : The salute of the Spanish republicans. It's beautiful because it isn't wicked like that . . .

Bruno *turns his fist through 90 degrees and back again.*

Bruno : . . . it's proud.

They pass a large house behind high iron gates.

Bruno : Hey, look, Jacques, did you know that is where Benjamin Constant and Madame de Stael lived?

Jacques : You were specially chosen to kill Palivoda to see if you were afraid.

Bruno : Fear, fear, I'm not afraid of anything. You're stupid. No, I don't want to, I won't do it.

Jacques : You'll be made to, old man.

Bruno : You'll never make me.

The Peugeot flashes past down a long desolate road.

Bruno *off :* Even a soldier can't be forced to kill someone.

Jacques : But what's the matter with you? Are you mad? It's easy! The Swiss know you're a deserter. The smallest slip, and they'll send you back to France.

Bruno *stares at* Jacques.

Bruno *off :* As long as I don't lower my eyes.

Jacques : And then, it's a Court Martial, and no one will help you get away, this time.

Paul : If you don't want to get rid of him, you'll take his place. Ask Jacques.

Bruno : So, you'll kill me.

Jacques : Twenty-six, that's very young to die, little prince.

Bruno *off :* If they force me to do it, okay, I'll kill Arthur Palivoda, but not before. There, that's what I said.

Close up : traffic lights at red.

Bruno : I'll leave you here. So long.

Bruno *gets out of the car and slams the door.*

Radio Message *over :* . . . *while we are on this subject another member of parliament, the member Beible for Seine and Oise wanted to go to Spanish Algeria while waiting . . . but he was deported and is at this moment in Palma, Majorca . . . those are the details we can give you in reply.*

JACQUES *watches him go and calls after him.*
JACQUES : So, I can rely on you?
BRUNO : No. Because I'm a bloody nuisance.
JACQUES : That's not at all funny.
 JACQUES *sits in the car staring out at* BRUNO. BRUNO *stands in the middle of the road, gives his clenched fist salute, and runs off down a tree-lined suburban street.*
BRUNO : I believed that the important thing in life was not to be defeated.
 Exterior. Night. BRUNO *is telephoning from a public call-box. His conversation is not heard but his narration continues.*
BRUNO *off :* Then, I can't remember what I did. Oh yes, I telephoned the Brazilian Consulate and asked how long it took to get a visa for one French boy and one Russian girl. But they were already closed. I will ring again tomorrow.
 Looking up from BRUNO'S *open car, the neon-lit facades of office buildings and shops slide by outlined against the night sky.* BRUNO'S *narration continues.*
BRUNO *off :* After that I made a tour of the town. The outline of buildings at night against a starry sky is always in some way moving, hard and mysterious, at the same time in the image of men and what lies beyond them.
 Close up : VERONICA *standing on the pavement, illuminated by street lights and shop windows, playing with her hair.*
BRUNO *off :* She pretended not to see me.
 From BRUNO'S *car the camera follows the leather-jacketed street photographer, as he suddenly rushes off*

*down the street, outlined against the lighted shop
windows.*

BRUNO *off* : But I didn't stop because I was frightened and,
anyway, I was seeing her the next day.

From BRUNO'S *car the camera tracks past boats on the
lake and then pans round to show a car following.*

BRUNO *off* : A little later, passing in front of Rousseau Island,
I noticed a car following me. I had to take several turnings
before I shook it off.

From BRUNO'S *car the camera pans left to show neon-
lit buildings reflected in the still waters of the lake. The
camera continues to pan until it looks straight ahead over*
BRUNO'S *shoulder. As he drives, an unlit cigarette
between his lips, he looks repeatedly to his left; there
is an expression of anxious surliness on his face.*

BRUNO *off* : Now ' everything is quiet. The enemy in the
shadow is resting.'

*Exterior. Daytime. From the top of a building the camera
looks down at a busy inter-section where cars pass back
and forth like insects. The camera pans slowly up to
show a park, the lake and a bridge.*

BRUNO *off* : Summer wasn't far off. People were bathing
already. And yet, to me it felt like winter.

Exterior. Daytime. A modern apartment block. BRUNO
draws up in his Chevrolet.

Close up : Photograph of VERONICA. PAUL *leans out of
the window of the Peugeot, examining it. Quick pan.*
BRUNO *walks into shot pulling a satchel of camera
equipment on to his shoulder. The camera follows him
as he walks up to the Peugeot.*

BRUNO : Hello, Paul, what are you doing here?

Without replying PAUL *drives off.* BRUNO, *puzzled,
watches him go, waves his hand in impatience and dis-
gust and enters the block of flats.*

A quick pan up the face of the building.

BRUNO *off :* Her place isn't bad.

> *Interior.* VERONICA'S *apartment. A stark room, painted all white with a small kitchen opening off it. There is a minimum of furniture; a divan bed, a couple of chairs, a table. Beside the front door a bookshelf acts as a room-divider, but the shelves have nothing on them. On the wall by the bed hangs a long mirror. There are no ornaments or visible possessions in the room. Venetian blinds shield the windows.* VERONICA *helps* BRUNO *off with his coat.*

VERONICA : Oh, there's nothing yet. I've just moved in.

BRUNO : No, no, it's not bad.

> VERONICA *stands in front of the mirror re-arranging her hair with her fingers, as* BRUNO *walks around taking readings with a light meter.*

BRUNO : It's funny, yesterday, I wasn't with you and I was thinking of you. Today, I am with you . . . and I'm thinking of other things.

> VERONICA *takes hold of the camera round* BRUNO'S *neck.*

VERONICA : Is that all you've got?

> *She begins combing her hair.*

VERONICA : I thought you needed masses of things, lamps . . .

> *As she talks,* BRUNO *starts taking photographs at machine gun speed.*

BRUNO : No, no, no, no, no, no. I've such sensitive film. It's Agfa Record. When you photograph a face . . . look at me . . .

> *Close up :* VERONICA *turns to face the camera.*
>
> BRUNO *puts a light meter up against her face.*

BRUNO : . . . you photograph the soul behind it.

> VERONICA *continues the incessant combing of her hair.*

BRUNO *off :* She has rings round her eyes. They were Velasquez grey.

VERONICA : Where would you like me to be?

BRUNO : Anywhere, er, anywhere.

As they continue to talk VERONICA *paces restlessly back-wards and forwards like a caged bird and then sits down on the bed and examines herself in a small hand mirror. Meanwhile,* BRUNO *takes photograph after photograph, occasionally taking another meter reading and adjusting his camera.*

BRUNO : It's all the same, it doesn't matter. You do what you like and I'll photograph you. I know, I'll ask you questions and you reply . . . that will be easy. You look scared, why?

VERONICA : Yes, I'm scared.

BRUNO : You mustn't be.

VERONICA : To me, it's as if the police were questioning me.

BRUNO *off :* She is less beautiful than yesterday afternoon.

BRUNO : Yes, yes, a little. Photography is truth . . . and the cinema is the truth twenty-four times a second. You're called Veronica what?

BRUNO *off :* She didn't reply straight away.

VERONICA : Veronica Dreyer.

VERONICA *gets up from the bed and walks across to the room-divider. She picks up a lens-hood and starts playing with it as she talks. She goes back to the mirror and commences the incessant re-arrangement of her hair. All the time* BRUNO *circles around her taking photographs.*

BRUNO : You are Finnish, oh no, Danish.

VERONICA : No, I'm Russian. But born in Copenhagen.

BRUNO : What are you doing in Geneva? You are with your parents.

VERONICA : No, I'm alone.

BRUNO *off :* A foreigner speaking French, it's always very attractive.

BRUNO : And your parents, where are they?

VERONICA : They were shot during the war.

BRUNO : Oh yes, who were they shot by?

VERONICA : That's none of your business.

BRUNO : By the Germans? By the Russians, then?

VERONICA : That's none of your business.

BRUNO : Why don't you want to tell me?

VERONICA : Just because, that's all.

BRUNO : Lift your hair with your hands.

Close up : BRUNO, *his camera to his eye.*

Close up : VERONICA *holding her hair up, looking into the camera with wide-open eyes and a mysterious smile.*

BRUNO *off :* Veronica's charm was all her own, the curve of her shoulders, the worry in her eyes, the secret of her smile.

BRUNO *continues taking photographs and changing lenses as he talks.*

BRUNO : That's funny, my father was shot, too. At the Liberation. He was a friend of Drieu la Rochelle.

Wearily BRUNO *rubs his eyes.* VERONICA *returns to comb her hair in front of the mirror. The camera stares steadily at her profile.*

BRUNO : Move a little, Veronica, don't stand there motionless.

VERONICA : What do you want me to do?

BRUNO : I don't know, do what you want, light a cigarette. Take a shower.

VERONICA : No. Why?

BRUNO *off :* Suddenly, she turned away.

BRUNO : You never take a shower?

BRUNO *off :* I was saying just anything to her.

BRUNO : I want to take some photographs of you taking a shower. You really don't want to?

VERONICA : No.

BRUNO : Why not?

VERONICA : Because I think it's stupid.

BRUNO : Are you frightened of me seeing your body? What were you going to say? What are you thinking about at this moment? Move about a bit.

The camera follows VERONICA *as she walks around the room.*

BRUNO : Do you ever think of death?

40

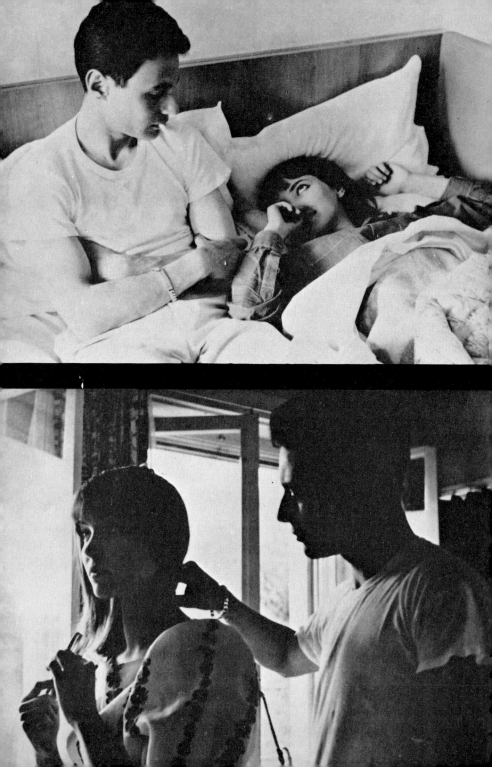

Close up : Bruno *taking photographs as he follows her around.*

Bruno *off :* She gave me a look of anguish . . .

Close up : Veronica *staring straight at the camera.*

Bruno *off :* . . . and, suddenly, I had the extraordinary feeling of photographing death. Then everything was normal once more.

Close up : Veronica.

Bruno : And since you have been in Geneva, have lots of boys been chasing you?

Veronica : Yes . . . why do you ask?

She smiles and goes back to combing her hair as Bruno *walks restlessly around. As they talk the camera seems to be probing into* Veronica, *waiting for her to reveal herself.*

Bruno : Oh, just wanted to know. I'm sure you've already posed for photographs in a swim-suit.

Veronica : No. Never.

Bruno : There, now, what are you thinking? Are you thinking about me?

Veronica : Yes.

Bruno : What do you think of me? Why don't you answer? I would almost say you were frightened. Put your hair behind your ears. Just a moment, put that record thing in front of your face.

Veronica *picks up a cardboard record sleeve and looks through the hole in the centre.*

Bruno : Do you believe in freedom.

Veronica : No.

Bruno : Would you be afraid to kill someone?

Veronica : Oh, you annoy me.

Bruno : Have you any brothers and sisters?

Veronica : Yes, one brother.

Bruno : What does he do?

VERONICA : He's in Moscow. He's a student at the Stanislavsky Theatre.

BRUNO : The Russians. They're always studying.

VERONICA : What?

BRUNO : The Russians. They're always studying.

VERONICA sits at a bare wooden table on which stands a vase with a single tulip. In the background white walls and a white radiator.

BRUNO : It's funny, you wanting to be an actress.

VERONICA opens a packet of cigarettes, takes one out and lights it.

BRUNO *off :* She lit a cigarette and asked why.

VERONICA : Why?

BRUNO : Actors. It's stupid to me. I despise them. It's true, you tell them to laugh, they laugh.

BRUNO grins at the camera with hideous falsity.

BRUNO : You tell them to cry, they cry. You tell them to crawl, they do it. To me, that's grotesque.

VERONICA : I don't see why.

BRUNO : I don't know, they're not free men.

As they are talking VERONICA has picked up a book, and leafing through it she walks over to BRUNO.

VERONICA : Look.

Close up : Reproduction of a painting in the book.

VERONICA : An actor.

BRUNO : Oh yes, it's a Klee.

BRUNO turns the pages.

BRUNO : You like Paul Klee?

VERONICA goes back to the mirror and once more starts playing with her hair. BRUNO puts down the book.

VERONICA : Yes.

BRUNO : What's important is not the way others see you . . . it's the way you see yourself.

VERONICA : Was it Paul Klee who said that?

BRUNO : No, it was me.

> BRUNO *stares at himself in the mirror and then turns towards* VERONICA.

BRUNO : Got any records?

> VERONICA *holds up a glossy record sleeve.*

VERONICA : Yes. What do you want? Some Bach . . .

> BRUNO *looks at his watch.*

BRUNO : No. It's too late. Bach is for 8 o'clock in the morning . . . a Brandenberg at 8 o'clock in the morning is wonderful.

> VERONICA *holds up another sleeve.*

VERONICA : Some Mozart? Beethoven?

> BRUNO *reloads his camera.*

BRUNO : Too early. Mozart is 8 o'clock at night. Beethoven is very profound music. Beethoven is midnight. No, what is needed is . . . just a moment, some Haydn.

> *The music starts.* VERONICA *dances round the room as* BRUNO *photographs her. Into the kitchen she goes, twirling round, up on the bed and down again. Finally, she lifts off the pick-up head. The music stops and she sinks exhausted into a chair.* BRUNO *continues to take photographs.*

BRUNO : What are you thinking about?

> *The camera pans to* VERONICA *and back to* BRUNO.

VERONICA : The same thing as you.

BRUNO : Do you know what a Rorschach is? It's a small drawing for telling people's character. I'll get you to do one.

> BRUNO *takes out a pen and notebook and starts to draw.*

BRUNO *off :* This is something I often do with women.

> *Close up :* BRUNO'S *hand draws a triangle, a circle and a square.*

BRUNO *off :* They love you to call them little girl, and ask them to play children's games.

> BRUNO *passes the notebook and the pen to* VERONICA.

BRUNO : Do what you like, anything at all. You finish the drawing, that's all.

Close up : Veronica *turns the square into a toy-soldier's head and the circle into a girl with pig-tails, while they are talking.*

Bruno : Did Hugh tell you about the bet we made yesterday afternoon?

Veronica : When you gave him 50 dollars? No.

Bruno : You don't know why I gave him 50 dollars?

Veronica : No.

She passes the notebook back to Bruno.

Veronica : You do one as well. I would like to know what you are thinking.

Bruno : I'll show you.

Bruno *turns the triangle, the circle and the square into the words I LOVE YOU.*

Exterior. Night. A neon sign HOTEL CENTURY against the darkness. The camera pans down to show the Peugeot parked by the kerb. Bruno *and* Veronica *drive up in the Chevrolet and get out.*

Bruno *off :* Jacques' and Paul's Peugeot was parked with its lights out in front of the Century. I pretended not to see them. Veronica and I, in the Chevrolet, talked about painting. She maintained that Van Gogh was a less great painter than Gauguin . . . which isn't true, of course.

Paul *and* Jacques *sit in their darkened car.* Paul *lights a cigarette.* Jacques *winds down the window.*

Jacques : There he is. But who is the girl?

Paul : A cover-girl.

Radio Message *over :* . . . *there is a general strike . . . crumble . . . barricades have been erected in the open . . .*

Bruno *and* Veronica *stand outlined against a lighted showroom window.* Bruno *lights a cigarette.*

Bruno : Are you staying with me, Veronica, or not?

48

VERONICA: I don't know, I don't know, Bruno.

BRUNO: Coming out of the 58 Club, you took my arm.

VERONICA: Shouldn't I have? Why?

VERONICA *leans with her back against the showroom window.* BRUNO *puts the palms of his hands flat against the window, one on either side of* VERONICA'S *face, so she is trapped between his outstretched arms.*

BRUNO: Because it made me want to go to bed with you. Now you seem to be saying it's not on. You shouldn't give your arm to a man if you don't want to do anything with him.

BRUNO *turns and walks off.*

BRUNO: Good-bye.

VERONICA *gazes wistfully after him.* JACQUES *who is watching, lights a cigarette.* VERONICA *runs after* BRUNO, *takes his arm and they disappear into the Century Hotel.* PAUL *gets out of the Peugeot.*

RADIO MESSAGE *over*: *It is a revolution . . . it was a very great empire, it was a very great empire, that had no, no, never abdicated, rah, rah.*

PAUL: You think it will work?

JACQUES: Yes, Bruno is a coward.

PAUL *smashes the window of* BRUNO'S *car, opens the door and gets in. The Peugeot drives off into the darkness followed by the Chevrolet.*

A city street at night. Headlights passing. Street lights.

BRUNO *off*: Then Paul took the wheel of my car. He and Jacques had put their threats into practice and thought up a way to put the Swiss police on to me.

PAUL *drives the Chevrolet straight at a parked car and then drives off into the darkness. The owner of the smashed car runs out of a nearby café, shouting.*

MARECHAL: My Pontiac! You bastard, hey, my Pontiac!

Stop him, stop him, police!

Interior. Close up : News photographs of the Hungarian revolution. The camera pans on to show a copy of Malraux's THE HUMAN CONDITION, then back up to more photographs of violence, a cinema poster of Bardot, a photo of a boxer with blood streaming down his face. Finally the camera comes to rest on BRUNO'S *face. He is wearing a white T-shirt, is unshaven and smoking a cigarette.*

BRUNO *off :* It's a German song. Would you like me to translate it for you, Veronica?

' O shining dawn, shining dawn,

too soon you tell me of my death . . .

soon the trumpets will sound . . .

. . . and then . . .

. . . I must leave this oh so beautiful life.'

BRUNO looks up desperately. The camera pans across more photographs. Like the others, they are stuck to the bare white wall above BRUNO'S *bed. Over images of war and pin-ups indiscriminately jumbled,* BRUNO'S *narration continues.*

BRUNO *off :* 7 a.m. Several quick snaps taken at the four corners of the world passed before me, like a bad dream! Panama, Rome, Alexandria, Budapest, Paris. The bad dream continues. ' We went to war as, when children, we went to school.' These were the first words in one of Bernanos' books. I remember the title : ' Humiliated Children.'

The camera again comes to rest on BRUNO'S *face as he looks up at the photographs. He lights his cigarette with a lighter.*

BRUNO *off :* I relit my cigarette. In fact, this morning I felt deep down just like a little boy. Why? Perhaps after all asking questions is more important than finding answers.

VERONICA lies beside BRUNO *in the bed, her arm over her eyes. She turns to look up at him.*

50

VERONICA : Give me a drag.

> BRUNO *puts his cigarette in her mouth.* VERONICA *draws on it.*

VERONICA : Oh, I'm hungry.

> VERONICA *sits up and then flops back on to the pillow. She digs her face into the pillow trying to get back to sleep as* BRUNO *talks.*

BRUNO : I had a nightmare. I dreamt I was going to the theatre . . . and I met the devil during the interval . . . and he was very well dressed. But it really was the devil . . . with hairy legs and horns . . .

> *As he talks he picks up a flick knife from the bedside table, opens it and holds the point to his palm.*

BRUNO : . . . and he was wounded in the thigh . . . a great red gash. It was horrible!

> *A knock on the door.*

BRUNO : Yes, who's that?

> BRUNO *leaps from the bed and snatches a gun from the drawer in the bedside table.*

VERONICA : Where are you going?

BRUNO : Nowhere. Go to sleep.

> *Close up :* VERONICA.

BRUNO *off :* God, she was beautiful!

> BRUNO *goes into the bathroom and comes back without the gun.*

> *Close up :* VERONICA.

BRUNO *off :* I wondered if she was pretending to sleep.

> BRUNO *stands by the half-open door of his hotel room talking to a man in a dark overcoat.*

INSPECTOR : Police. You are Bruno Forestier?

BRUNO : Yes. What's the matter?

INSPECTOR : Put on your jacket and come with me.

BRUNO : No. I've done nothing.

INSPECTOR : You know, you'll do better not to get clever with us; you're wanted in France.

Bruno: Yes, I'm a deserter. But here, I'm clean.

Inspector: Just put on your jacket. We'll see about that.

Bruno reaches for his jacket.

Exterior. In the street it has been raining.

Bruno crosses the road between the Inspector and a uniformed Gendarme. He turns up the collar of his jacket, puts a cigarette in his mouth and lights it as the Inspector talks.

Bruno *off :* You ran away, that's serious, said the Inspector. If the fellow brings a charge against you, you'll be expelled from Geneva . . . and as a deserter, handed over to the French authorities.

The three men approach Bruno's car, parked by the kerb. They examine the damage.

Bruno *off :* As I didn't yet know what the trouble was, I began by denying everything.

Inspector: There, take a good look.

Bruno crouches and tries to straighten the damaged bumper. The Inspector beckons to some people across the road. The camera follows his gesture and shows the Peugeot parked there. A man in dark glasses (Marechal) gets out. It is the man Bruno asked for a light on the train. As he crosses the road, the Inspector turns to Bruno.

Inspector: Just because you're French you don't have to run off.

Bruno: I didn't run off. I wasn't there.

Marechal joins them.

Marechal: Oh, so he's French. I'm not surprised, these bloody Frenchmen think they can do anything!

Inspector: Well, were you there, or weren't you?

The camera pans to Bruno, a cigarette drooping from his lips. He looks surly and hang-dog.

Bruno *off :* Never lower your head in front of the police.

Bruno lowers his head and shakes it, indicating no.

INSPECTOR : You don't know?

BRUNO *off :* What a fool I was! Too late!

INSPECTOR : But this gentleman has witnesses.

MARECHAL : They are there, in the car.

> MARECHAL *points across the road.* JACQUES *and* PAUL *are sitting in the Peugeot.*

BRUNO *off :* I understood too late. This was the promised trouble if I didn't kill Palivoda.

> *The camera pans from the* GENDARME *to the* INSPECTOR *to* BRUNO *and then to* MARECHAL.

GENDARME : Right, shall I get back to my beat?

BRUNO *off :* I had lost my first serious battle.

INSPECTOR *to* MARECHAL : Well, are you bringing a charge or not?

> MARECHAL *looks across at* JACQUES. JACQUES *indicates no by shaking his head and stares at* BRUNO.

BRUNO *off :* A deep feeling of loneliness flooded over me. But maybe remorse . . .

> BRUNO *stares back at* JACQUES.

BRUNO *off :* . . . is the start of freedom.

> BRUNO *bites his lips and stares at the ground. Then he nods his assent towards* JACQUES.
> *Close up :* BRUNO *ascending in a lift.*
> *Ominous piano chords.*
> BRUNO *stares at his reflection in the glass of the lift door. The lift stops. He gets out.*
> *In* BRUNO'S *room* VERONICA, *dressed in a girlish, full-skirted cotton dress, is doing her hair.*
> BRUNO *enters, taking off his jacket and throwing it on to a chair. In the background a radio plays.*

RADIO MESSAGE *over :* . . . *it isn't a man alone . . . are sent back . . . one asks oneself . . . amid the tumult you understand four words of the reply: we take up arms.*

VERONICA: Where have you been?

BRUNO: To buy some cigarettes.

BRUNO *starts to pull on a sweater.*

BRUNO: Have you had a bath?

VERONICA: No. I didn't feel like it.

BRUNO *grasps* VERONICA'S *hair in his fist and lifts it away from her neck.*

BRUNO: A woman's shoulders, they're very pretty and very noble.

VERONICA: You're very funny this morning.

BRUNO: Yes, I've become a coward.

VERONICA: What?

BRUNO *goes into the bathroom, pulling the sweater over his head. He looks at himself in the mirrored door of the medicine cupboard.* VERONICA, *standing at the door, is reflected in the mirror.*

BRUNO: I've become a coward. It's funny, when I look straight at my own face . . .

VERONICA *comes up beside him. They both look into the mirror.*

BRUNO: I feel it doesn't match the idea I have of myself from inside.

They look at each other.

BRUNO: In your opinion . . . which is the most important: the interior or the exterior?

VERONICA *kisses him on the cheek and goes into the bedroom.* BRUNO *opens the medicine cupboard.*

Close up : a revolver.

BRUNO *off :* It was a beautiful thing, black, mysterious, incorruptible.

BRUNO'S *hand picks it up and his finger curls round the trigger.*

Exterior. Day. The radio-station where JACQUES *and* PAUL *had pointed out* PALIVODA *to* BRUNO *the day before.*

RADIO MESSAGE: ■■ *where a flag flew stained with*

blood. It's now a week, day for day, hour for hour, since
the uprising took place . . . Air-France from ■■, this
Caravelle circled what is more for an hour over Orly
before landing because of bad weather . . . you can see
what a suspense that was . . . 24 dead 180 wounded,
police ■■ on one side, civilians, ■■ on the other . . .
why? . . . the unnerving of ■■ after 22 of them were
killed in two months in the plain of ■ ■, four months . . .*
PALIVODA *comes out, pulling on his jacket and gets into*
his Nash. Quick pan to the waiting Peugeot.
Close up : At the car window in the place of BRUNO'S *face*
we see the face of Hitler on the cover of L'EXPRESS.
A hand raises a revolver in front of Hitler's picture and
aims it.
The camera looks out of the car from behind BRUNO'S
head. He lowers the magazine and watches PALIVODA
half get out of his Nash as someone comes running up
to talk to him. On the Peugeot's radio we hear the voice
of PALIVODA.

Voice of PALIVODA *on radio :* It is exactly a week now to the
day, to the hour, since the massacres started.

The voice continues indistinctly. BRUNO *has missed his*
first chance of a shot. He puts down his gun and drives
off after PALIVODA.
The two cars stop at a level-crossing. The Peugeot pulls
alongside. BRUNO *aims carefully through the window.*
At that very moment a cyclist comes between them.
BRUNO *puts the gun away.*
The camera tracks after the two cars as the pursuit
continues down nondescript semi-country roads. BRUNO
tries to pull out and draw alongside. Just as he does so

---

* Translator's note. The black squares left in this and subsequent radio
messages were censored from the original sound-track by the French
authorities. As no script exists to a Godard film prior to shooting, this
is all taken direct from the sound-track.

PALIVODA, *too, has to pull out to avoid a parked car.*
BRUNO *off :* It was what my friend Raoul Coutard, the most brilliant of French cameramen, called the law of the greatest fuck-up.

BRUNO *tries again. This time there is a car approaching. He pulls back behind* PALIVODA.
BRUNO *off :* Each time I was ready to fire, an unforeseen incident stopped me.

Again BRUNO *pulls alongside and aims.*
BRUNO *off :* Each time the coast was clear, no witness . . . I hesitated a few seconds . . . and once again it was too late.

The camera tracks back in front of the two cars.
Once more BRUNO *pulls alongside.*
Close up : PALIVODA.
Close up : BRUNO *aiming.*
BRUNO *off :* I realized that it's difficult, if you're not a professional . . . trying to kill a man several times in succession.

A car pulls out of a side turning in front of BRUNO. *He is forced to stop.*
BRUNO *off :* It's like messing up a suicide attempt and then trying again.

BRUNO *gets out of his car as though to shout at the driver in his way. He seems to think better of it, gets back in and drives off down a straight, empty country road.*
A road beside the Lake of Geneva. In the foreground, public gardens. In the distance PALIVODA'S *car draws up at the kerb.* BRUNO'S *Peugeot pulls in ahead of it. Steady, monotonous piano music.*
Close up : BRUNO *looks round from the wheel.*
BRUNO *off :* After a little while, I had had enough of it.

BRUNO *looks through the back window and sees* PALIVODA *meeting a girl. They get into the Nash together. The pursuit continues through the streets of Geneva. The piano music continues.* PALIVODA *stops his car.* BRUNO *parks.* PALIVODA *walks across to a dark, small, wiry-looking man in dark glasses, who is standing in front of the Arabian Commercial Bank.*

BRUNO *off :* I don't think it was the business of killing someone. Although I hadn't done that often, I'd done it.

PALIVODA *shakes the man in dark glasses by the hand.*

PAUL *suddenly rushes up, gesturing to* BRUNO *to shoot.*

BRUNO *off :* No, it wasn't that . . . and conscientious objectors, for instance, I've always thought of them as scum.

PALIVODA *and his friend walk off examining a newspaper.*

BRUNO *off :* Then, what, old man?

BRUNO *gestures his refusal to* PAUL.

BRUNO *off :* Simply, there are things one does at certain moments of one's existence and at others one doesn't.

PAUL *rushes up and bundles* BRUNO *into the Peugeot. With* BRUNO *at the wheel they drive off. The monotonous piano music recommences.*

BRUNO *off :* Paul is always on the go; like a dog with a bone. And I, being so lazy, admire them, him and Jacques: never short of ideas. Real secret agents.

The Peugeot drives alongside the lake. PALIVODA *and his friend cross the lakeside promenade towards a jetty. The Peugeot parks. As* PALIVODA *talks to him, the man in dark glasses looks anxiously over his shoulder. It is a clear, sparkling, sunny day. Passers-by enjoy the sun-lit water and the warmth. Gulls gently wheel. But in this setting of happy normality* BRUNO *and* PAUL *stalk their prey.* PAUL *pats* BRUNO *on the back and gestures to him to get on with it.* BRUNO *walks forward, pulling a gun from his belt.* PAUL *follows.*

BRUNO *off :* Nothing puts them off, not even the stupidest things like making me assassinate Palivoda in front of 36 people.

The lake glints in the sunshine.

Close up : BRUNO *sitting on the ferry.*

57

PAUL *lights a cigarette. They look across at* PALIVODA *and his companion. A tourist takes a photo as the ferry crosses the lake.*

BRUNO *off :* Accused by friends of being a traitor, I could only get out of it by killing one of the enemy.

PALIVODA *hands something to his friend and they both get up ready to leave the boat.* BRUNO *gets up and stands behind them.*

BRUNO *off :* When I drew my revolver I felt Paul, at the same time, pointing his at me.

From the shore the camera follows PALIVODA *and his friend as they come up the landing stage. They are both writing in note books as they pass.* BRUNO *rushes after them, pushing the other passengers aside. Two friends of* BRUNO'S *happen to be passing. One shouts to him—*

HUGH : Bruno! How's your Danish girl?

PALIVODA'S *friend takes a photo of* BRUNO *with a miniature camera.* PAUL *rushes up the landing stage to join* BRUNO.

PAUL : Damn, they've got away.

A quick glimpse of PALIVODA *and his friend getting in a taxi.*

Close up : PAUL.

PAUL : You don't want to shoot. It's proof you're working for them!

PAUL *points his gun at* BRUNO. *Behind them the lake sparkles peacefully in the sunshine.*

BRUNO : Me? Not at all.

PAUL : Then what are you thinking of?

BRUNO : I'm fed up. To hell with you!

BRUNO *grabs at* PAUL'S *gun, pushes him into the lake and rushes off down the quayside.*

BRUNO *off :* Now, pursued by the French and unmasked by the Arabs, I was in for it twice over.

Close up : VERONICA *wearing dark glasses against a*

white wall is talking on the telephone.
VERONICA : No, I'm going to have a bath. Later, at the Club, the 58 Club, if you like . . . why?
Close up : BRUNO in a telephone kiosk.
BRUNO : I can't stay in Geneva. Tomorrow, I'm off to Zurich . . . I'm taking a plane to Brazil.
As he talks his eyes stare out, on guard.
BRUNO : Why aren't you saying anything?
VERONICA sits on the bed in her flat, the telephone on her lap.
VERONICA : I don't know what to say.
The camera pans across the room. There, playing chess, sit PALIVODA and his friend.
Close up : BRUNO in profile.
BRUNO : Lie to me . . . Say that you aren't sad that I am leaving.
Close up : VERONICA in profile.
VERONICA : I'm not sad that you are leaving. I'm not in love with you. I won't join you in Brazil. I don't kiss you tenderly.
The ominous, monotonous piano chords recommence.
VERONICA replaces the receiver, takes off her dark glasses and chews them as she thinks.
BRUNO *off :* So I packed quickly and headed for Zurich.
Dusk. BRUNO once more crosses the lake in his car.
BRUNO *off :* They were no longer the lights of Geneva, but already those of Rio de Janeiro . . . and I wondered if I was happy to feel free . . . or free to feel happy.
Ominous piano chords.
A road at night. BRUNO pulls into a filling station. Ahead of him a group of men get out of a large chauffeur-driven Cadillac. BRUNO goes into the garage office. He stands at the telephone waiting for a call.
Close up : The photograph of BRUNO taken that afternoon at the lake by PALIVODA'S friend. A pen rings

BRUNO'S *head and an unknown man examines the photo-*
graph. BRUNO *still waits for his call inside the garage.*
BRUNO : Hello, Jacques.
Interior of the office of the French News Agency.
PAUL : No, it's Paul.
PAUL *in shirt-sleeves passes the phone to* JACQUES, *who*
puts down his book and puts a gun on top of it. In the
background there is an indistinct voice on a radio.
JACQUES : You'd better watch out, you know, old man . . .
Oh yes, tragedy today is politics. No, that's not me, it's
Napoleon. Good, listen, Bruno . . . But let me . . . let me
speak . . .
BRUNO *stands, a small solitary figure, among a garage*
full of cars.
BRUNO : At any rate, I'm just ringing to tell you the Peugeot
is in front of the Century Hotel.
Close up : Ringed photo of BRUNO. *Two of the men from*
the Cadillac rush off into the darkness. The Cadillac
follows. As BRUNO *comes out of the garage office, he is*
set upon.
BRUNO *off :* My head hit the ground so hard it knocked me
out.
BRUNO *is dragged off by the feet. One of the pump*
attendants tries to come to his rescue. He is held off
with a gun. BRUNO *is shoved into the Cadillac, which*
drives off. Ominous piano music.
The Cadillac speeds through the neon-lit streets.

RADIO MESSAGE *over :* at ■ ■, *there are determined men . . .*
men determined to make the supreme sacrifice . . . men
determined to die to remain ■ ■ *. . . it is a powder-puff . . .*
long live ■ ■ *! . . . Paris will deny . . .*

BRUNO, *blind-folded, is brought into a dimly lit room and*
dumped on the floor. One of his captors is PALIVODA'S

60

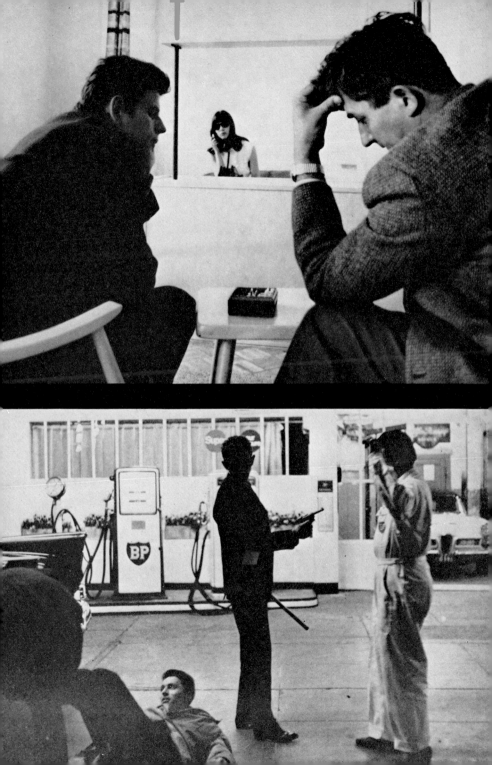

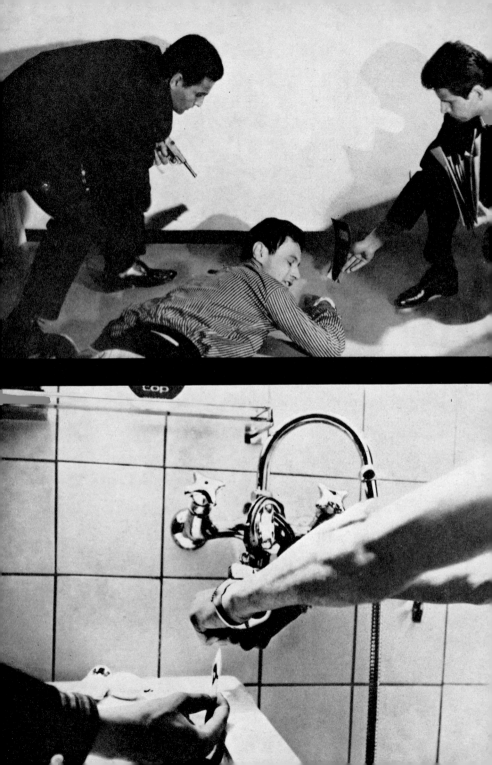

friend, LASZLO.

BRUNO *off :* I forgot to count the steps to know what floor we were on.

LASZLO'S *aides take off* BRUNO'S *handcuffs and blind- fold and dump him in a chair.* LASZLO *turns on a tape- recorder.*

LASZLO : In the garage, who were you ringing?

BRUNO : Are you going to torture me?

LASZLO : Are you frightened?

BRUNO : Of course, I'm frightened.

An aid takes out BRUNO'S *passport, looks at it and hands it to* LASZLO, *who examines it with care.*

LASZLO : Who made you this passport? The French consulate here?

BRUNO : I remember an Arab story : it's about a guy who picks up the phone and says, ' Allo? ' Someone answers, ' No, it's Ali.'

One of LASZLO'S *aids, a tough, handsome Arab called* MOHAMMED, *asks:*

MOHAMMED : Shall we undress him?

LASZLO *examines a file full of photographs. On the wall behind him is a map. He nods.*

BRUNO *off :* If I had shouted, they would have knocked me out again. Better accept the fight.

MOHAMMED *starts to strip* BRUNO, *while* LASZLO *shows him a photograph.*

LASZLO : Who is this?

Close up : Photograph of BEAUREGARD.

BRUNO : I don't know.

LASZLO *shows* BRUNO *another photograph.*

LASZLO : And this one?

BRUNO : Never seen him.

BRUNO *turns away his head.* MOHAMMED *turns it roughly back again.*

Close up : Photograph of JACQUES.

LASZLO *off :* Jacques Aurélien Mercier, Indochina volunteer. We lost track of him during the Piastre smuggling affair. We caught up with him in '57 in Rotterdam, when the cargo ship *Aramis* blew up. In '59, in Frankfurt, when Professor Dietrich was assassinated . . . and now in Geneva.

> LASZLO *puts the photograph in his folder.* MOHAMMED *takes off* BRUNO'S *jacket and pins his arms behind his back with handcuffs.* LASZLO *continues the interrogation.*

LASZLO : Was it him you were ringing?

> *He begins to shout.*

LASZLO : What was the number?

> *The camera pans across the face of the building. An occasional lighted window shines out of the blackness of the largely darkened building.*

BRUNO *off :* Contrary to what you think, I don't mind telling you. But I don't want to. I won't. That's what I told them. They suggested I work for them.

> BRUNO *is now sitting on the floor, his back against the wall.* MOHAMMED *kicks him back onto the floor.*

BRUNO *off :* I asked them for some money in advance. They didn't want to. So, I told them to get lost.

> *Close up : Photograph of a blood-spattered face.*

LASZLO : He too, Alfred Latouche . . . he refused to speak.

> *A photograph of another scarred, battered face is placed on top of the first.*

LASZLO : And that's his brother Etienne.

> *Close up :* BRUNO *looks at the photographs.*

LASZLO : Want us to do the same to you?

BRUNO *off :* Poor Etienne. He must have lowered his head so as not to get his throat cut. Result, he got the razor right across the chin.

> MOHAMMED *takes the photographs and looks at them.*

MOHAMMED : I hope you are brave.

> *A lighted cigarette dangles from one corner of his mouth as he talks.*

MOHAMMED: It's going to be tough.

BRUNO *looks down.*

BRUNO: I don't know if I'm brave, but I'll soon see.

LASZLO: We'll just have to put him in the bathroom.

LASZLO *tidies up his files and, taking out his portable chess set, sits down at his desk.* MOHAMMED *drags* BRUNO *out of the room by one foot. As* LASZLO *dials a number,* MOHAMMED'S *voice can be heard talking roughly to* BRUNO.

MOHAMMED: Get up!

LASZLO *looks up as* MOHAMMED *comes back into the room, closing the door.*

The camera pans across the darkened face of the building.

BRUNO *off :* ' You slip ever further from the living. Soon they will have struck you from their lists. That is the only way to share the privileges of the dead. What privileges? To die no longer.'

The bathroom is harshly lit from its central light. It glitters ruthlessly with tile, mirror and chromium. LASZLO *covers* BRUNO *with his revolver as* MOHAMMED *stretches him out, one arm manacled to the wash basin, the other to a towel rail. Then* MOHAMMED *begins to spray* BRUNO'S *face with a hand-shower.*

The camera pans across the face of the building, which is now sunlit.

BRUNO *off :* Torture, it's monotonous and sad. It is difficult to talk about, so I will say very little.

Ominous piano music. MOHAMMED *comes out of the bathroom combing his hair. Patting his stomach, he jokes with* LASZLO *about their waist-lines. In the living room a dark* GIRL *wearing a black sweater, her hair cropped close to her neat head, sits at a typewriter.*

In the bathroom LASZLO *holds a tiny transistor to his ear and then puts it down on the basin.*

67

LASZLO : What number were you ringing?

BRUNO, *spreadeagled, stares doggedly up at* LASZLO *as he lights a cigarette.*

LASZLO : Are you scared?

BRUNO : Why are you doing this?

LASZLO : You must have the strength sometimes to cut your way with a dagger.

Close up: The GIRL *in the living room is reading Mao tse-Tung's 'A SPARK CAN SET FIRE TO THE WHOLE PLAIN.'* LASZLO *lights his cigarette with a bunch of five matches and then holds them under* BRUNO'S *manacled wrist.* BRUNO *tries to pull his hand away.*

Close up : LASZLO *retunes his transistor.* BRUNO *thrashes about, trying to escape the flame.*

BRUNO *off :* In Budapest, I had already seen people tortured. I remember I asked myself if I would be able to hold out. So now this was it.

LASZLO : To the basin.

MOHAMMED *handcuffs* BRUNO *to the wash-basin taps.*

BRUNO *off :* I know they've done much worse to others. But martyred comrades met in the corridors . . .

In the living room the GIRL *continues to type and answer the telephone.*

BRUNO *off :* . . . the screams through the walls. I didn't have that.

Close up : BRUNO'S *handcuffed wrists being burnt with matches.*

BRUNO *off :* So I can't talk about that.

Close up : BRUNO'S *tired, unshaven face. His head twists back and forth and ends staring at the camera.*

BRUNO *off :* All I know is that I forced myself not to cry out, and that, very quickly, I stopped struggling. Think of something else, go on, quickly, anything, avoid the pain, quick, the sea, the beach, the sun. Think so fast you're no longer thinking of anything. Write to Veronica, quick, quick, stop thinking of the pain. Quick, write a letter, always quicker, beat pain with speed. Veronica, a letter even more beautiful than the one from Robert Desnos to his wife.

BRUNO *is crouching in the bath. His face is being sprayed with the hand-shower. His head flops back against the wall and he splutters.*

BRUNO : What happened?

MOHAMMED : You fainted.

BRUNO : Did I cry?

MOHAMMED : Why do you ask?

LASZLO *comes in and sits on the edge of the bath.*

LASZLO : What's going on?

MOHAMMED : It's funny, he is asking if he cried. I wonder why that interests him?

The camera pans from MOHAMMED *to* LASZLO *to* BRUNO. *There is a long pause.*

BRUNO : Because it's important.

BRUNO *rests his head on his arms.*

BRUNO *off :* Between two sessions of torture, we had great political discussions. They thought I was completely idiotic to resist as I had no ideals, and then like any self-respecting revolutionary organization, they tried to indoctrinate me.

LASZLO *sits on the edge of the bath, a book in his hands.*

LASZLO : Your friends torture as well.

He begins to read.

LASZLO *reading :* 'Prisoners waited in darkness either for prison or an attempted escape, that is to say, a burst of machine-gun fire in the back.'

He looks at BRUNO.

LASZLO : Djamilla's fiancé died that way.

Close up: The GIRL *in the living room. She is reading Lenin.*

There is a knock on the door.

MOHAMMED *pushes* BRUNO'S *head under water as*

69

LASZLO *goes to answer the door.*

BRUNO *off* : As I couldn't stand it any longer, I screamed for help. But I didn't realize that I was so weak I couldn't be heard two yards away. I thought I was shouting when in fact I was speaking in a whisper.

> MOHAMMED *shoves* BRUNO *under water again and kicks the bathroom door shut.* LASZLO *opens the front door. It is a girl with the laundry.*
>
> *Monotonous piano music.* LASZLO, *smiling, takes the laundry and pays for it.*
>
> *Close up :* BRUNO, *still handcuffed, lies in the bath.*

BRUNO *off* : I wondered what the pile of shirts he put on the corner of the basin were for.

> *In the living room* MOHAMMED *lights a cigarette and ruffles* DJAMILLA'S *hair.*
>
> *Close up : A shirt is put over* BRUNO'S *head, pulled tight across his face and soaked with water.*
>
> *In the living room* LASZLO *talks on the telephone.*

LASZLO : Hallo, Palivoda, it's Cavalier F.4.

> *Close up :* MOHAMMED *continues to soak the shirt over* BRUNO'S *face.*

BRUNO *off* : Once the material is completely soaked with water, air no longer comes through, so it is impossible to breathe.

> *The cloth puffs up as* BRUNO *tries to breathe. He struggles to escape the water. He fights for breath.*
>
> *In the living room* LASZLO *is reading from a book into his tape-recorder.*

LASZLO *reading* : 'The revolutionary thrust is like a ship already visible on the far-off horizon. It is like the disc of the sun, whose burning rays already pierce the shadows. It is like the child who will soon see the light of day.'

> LASZLO *stops the recorder and turns to* MOHAMMED *who is sitting beside him.*

LASZLO : Has he told us the number?

70

Mohammed: No, no, still nothing, but with this, we'll get something.

Mohammed *waves a cut-throat razor.*

Laszlo: No, no, no. We musn't leave any marks.

Laszlo *runs the tape back.*

Close up : Bruno *tries to slide a razor-blade along the bathroom shelf with his chin, so he can reach it with his fingers.*

Bruno *off :* Why did I want to kill myself? I would have done better to tell them what they wanted.

In the living room.

Laszlo: That's the way the French got a bad reputation.

He listens to his recording.

Bruno's *fingers reach the razor-blade, he picks it up and puts it in his mouth.*

Bruno *off :* I took the blade in my teeth, as I couldn't manage it with my hands.

Laszlo *continues to listen to his recording.*

Bruno *starts to saw at his wrists with the razor-blade.*

Bruno *off :* Unluckily or luckily for me, they came into the bathroom before I succeeded.

The camera pans across the face of the building.

Bruno *off :* And then . . . now for the electric shock treatment.

A man in dark glasses and shirt-sleeves brings a box full of equipment into the living room. Bruno, *handcuffed, his jacket on, squats on the floor.*

Bruno *off :* A man I knew brought the equipment. Now I remember. It was the man who was giving a little dog to Veronica the first time we met.

Laszlo: Is it working, then, this time?

Bruno *off :* The electric shock treatment is very simple. They fix electrodes to any part of your body and pass the current through you. You never die, but it doesn't do you any good.

As Bruno *watches, they test the equipment and then fix*

71

the electrodes to his bare feet. DJAMILLA *listens to a transistor radio. The monotonous, ominous piano music breaks in.*

LASZLO : Remember what Lenin said : ' In the revolution, there are no " easy " tasks, no " easy " ways of fighting.'

Close up : The hand generator is turned. BRUNO *jerks round the room, beating the floor as the shocks hit him.* LASZLO'S *voice continues.*

LASZLO : ' This political line must be followed without exception on every front. The victory of the revolution is certain. It will triumph.'

Close up : The generator being turned very fast. Night again. The camera pans across the face of the building where once more a few lighted windows break the darkness.

BRUNO *off :* Then, they ordered me to put my clothes back on. I couldn't take any more.

BRUNO *dresses while* LASZLO, *sitting at a table, plays listlessly with his revolver.*

BRUNO *off :* Suddenly, I thought of throwing myself out of the window. If it was the first floor, all the better. If not . . .

MOHAMMED *puts* BRUNO'S *handcuffs on again.*

LASZLO : What are you thinking about?

BRUNO : I am thinking about Pierre Brossolette. I was told about his death. It was in '43 at the Gestapo place in the Rue Lauriston.

BRUNO *gets up and, holding his manacled hands in front of him, walks slowly round the room as he talks.* LASZLO *covers him with his gun. The camera follows* BRUNO.

BRUNO : They tortured him for two months. They put his eyes out. One day they led him into a room for a new interrogation.

BRUNO *begins to act out his story, feeling the white walls with his manacled hands.*

BRUNO : And Brossolette felt he had suffered so much, he

72

wouldn't be able to stop himself talking any longer. He felt that there was a window in the room. So, while they were questioning him, he edged towards it, bit by bit, feeling his way, and as soon as he touched the glass . . .

BRUNO pauses, his head sunk on his arms, his back to the camera. Then suddenly he swivels and throws himself at the window.

BRUNO : . . . he threw himself through it.

Two shots ring out.

Daylight. Slow pan down the face of the apartment block where VERONICA lives.

BRUNO *off :* We always have the luck we deserve. It was the first floor. I went and hid at Veronica's. She told me she was working for the Arabs, but if I was going to Brazil, she would escape with me.

Bright sunshine. VERONICA rushes up to the entrance of the block of apartments. She drops something in the road. As she stoops to pick it up, PAUL comes up to her.

PAUL : Excuse me, you still haven't seen my friend Forestier?

VERONICA : No.

VERONICA shakes her head and PAUL rejoins JACQUES who is leaning against their parked car. PAUL points up at the apartments.

PAUL : I'm sure he's there.

JACQUES : Why? She would tell us.

PAUL : I don't trust her.

A quick glimpse of VERONICA as she disappears into the hallway of the building. Quick pan up the face of the building.

VERONICA stands in the kitchen unwrapping a package. The monotonous piano music breaks in again. VERONICA has bought a key. She comes into the sitting room and starts to unlock BRUNO's handcuffs.

VERONICA : Why would you rather die than talk?

73

VERONICA *walks away as* BRUNO *finishes unlocking his handcuffs.*

BRUNO: They would have killed me anyway. Yes, after all, I don't know, no. Luckily it was the first floor, that's all. You look much better without make-up.

VERONICA *sits in the sunlight by the open window, takes out a cigarette and lights it.*

BRUNO *off :* I watched her sit down. I love the way she lights a cigarette.

VERONICA: It isn't true.

BRUNO *looks at her, gets up and starts pacing round the room swinging the handcuffs.*

BRUNO: It is. Why is it all empty?

VERONICA: Because I was leaving. I was off.

VERONICA *puts a cigarette in* BRUNO'S *mouth and lights it.*

BRUNO *off :* We didn't dare look at each other.

VERONICA *takes* BRUNO'S *chin in her hand, lifts his head and twists it from side to side. Then she looks inside his T-shirt.*

VERONICA: But nothing shows.

BRUNO: No, the burns a bit, here. But they take a lot of care. Since the Algerian question came up at the U.N. they must have received orders from Cairo. No one came and asked you where I was?

VERONICA *smoking, looks at herself in the mirror and re-arranges her hair with quick flicks of her fingers. She turns towards* BRUNO.

VERONICA: Yes, when I came back I passed your friends again.

Close up : BRUNO *smoking.*

BRUNO: Who do you mean?

VERONICA *walks about talking straight at the camera.*

VERONICA: They've already been here, yesterday, from the French consulate. The thin one looks like a lift boy and the

74

other one's like a gigolo. Who are they?

BRUNO : They are Paul and Jacques. Yes, yes, definitely.

BRUNO *sits down on the bed.*

BRUNO : It was us who assassinated Lachenal.

VERONICA *turns and walks away across the room.*

BRUNO *off :* Why has she turned her back on me?

VERONICA : No, that was stupid, I think. Palivoda, yes, but Lachenal hadn't done anything.

VERONICA *lets the window blind down a short way. Ominous piano music breaks in again.*

VERONICA : He thought the Algerian war was unjust, but that's all.

VERONICA *sits beside* BRUNO *as he makes a telephone call.*

BRUNO : Yes, I don't know.

VERONICA : You always say that.

The office of the French News Agency. JACQUES, *smoking a pipe, listens to* BRUNO *on the telephone.*

JACQUES : Of course, I'm listening.

He signals to PAUL *who starts writing on a sheet of paper with a felt pen.*

JACQUES : Mohammed Messoussa, 16 Chemin Chapellit. Where can I call you back? You don't want me to, why? Okay, old man, you call us.

JACQUES *puts down the telephone.*

BRUNO *off :* In exchange for two diplomatic passports I gave them the Arabs' address.

JACQUES *picks up the telephone and, as he dials, turns to* PAUL.

JACQUES : Paul, tell the little photographer to go and see.

The piano music continues. JACQUES *speaks into the telephone.*

JACQUES : Say, in your files, you've nothing on a girl called . . .

PAUL *looks at the name on the back of a photograph of* VERONICA.

PAUL : Ve . . . Veronica Dreyer?

75

JACQUES : You'll call me back?

JACQUES *replaces the receiver.*

Close up : VERONICA *sitting, fiddling with her hair.*

VERONICA : And me, then.

BRUNO : Why are you working with Palivoda's friends? From political conviction?

VERONICA : It's hard to say. Bit by bit.

Close up : BRUNO *looking down at her.*

VERONICA : But it doesn't worry me. Anyway, I found that the French were in the wrong . . .

Close up : VERONICA.

VERONICA : The others, they've got an ideal . . .

As she talks VERONICA *fiddles continuously with her cardigan.*

VERONICA : You must have an ideal, it's very important.

Against the Germans, the Fre . . . the French had an ideal.

VERONICA *gets up and flicks her cardigan over* BRUNO'S *head.*

VERONICA : Now they haven't, they'll lose the war.

VERONICA *covers her head with the cardigan.*

BRUNO : You think so? I don't.

VERONICA *takes the cardigan off her head and begins to pace about.*

VERONICA : Yes, they will.

BRUNO *gets up and walks over to* VERONICA.

BRUNO : It's funny, today, everyone detests the French. Me, I'm very proud to be French, but at the same time, I am against nationalism. It's ideas we defend, not territories . .

As he talks the camera follows BRUNO *around the room.*

BRUNO : . . . I love France, because I love Joachim du Bellay and Louis Aragon. I love Germany, because I love Beethoven. I don't love Barcelona because of Spain, but I love Spain because a town like Barcelona exists, or America because I love American cars, and I don't love the Arabs because I don't love the desert or Colonel Lawrence. Still less the Medi-

76

terranean and Albert Camus. No, I love Brittany and I detest
the south . . .

>BRUNO *pulls down a slat of the venetian blind and looks
out.*

BRUNO : . . . In Brittany the light is always very soft; not like
in the south . . . and then, the Arabs are lazy . . . ˙

>*Close up :* VERONICA *examining herself in the mirror.
She looks at* BRUNO *thoughtfully.*

BRUNO : . . . but I have nothing against them, nor the Chinese.
No, I would like to ignore them. But it's terrible today. If
you stay quietly doing nothing, you are cursed just because
you are doing nothing. So, we do things without conviction and I think it's a pity to make war without conviction . . .

>VERONICA *has a cigarette in her mouth. Just as she is
about to light it,* BRUNO *takes it and puts it in his own
mouth. Talking all the time he continues to pace around
the room.*

BRUNO : . . . Why is the Vatican against Communism? He's
funny, the Pope, and they both have the same idea, all men
are brothers. I'm not the brother of a tram driver in Peking,
nor in San Francisco. On the contrary, a priori, I couldn't
care less about him. Maybe one day it will interest me to
know what he is up to. But he isn't my brother and my friend
automatically . . . because he has eyes and ears like me . . .
and vice-versa. There are objects, I don't know. Some you
like, others you don't. Or colours. For example, I don't like
dark red. With men, it's the same. You can't be forced to love
them all, or else, it's what Sacha Guitry said : ' You no longer
know where to commit your heart.'

>*Close up :* BRUNO *ends his pacing, staring down at*
VERONICA.

>*Close up :* VERONICA, *smoking, thoughtful.*

BRUNO *off :* She looked at me. In my opinion, women should
never pass twenty-five.

>*As* BRUNO *continues to talk he moves restlessly around*

the room, moving from a chair to sit with VERONICA *on the bed and then continuing to pace around.* VERONICA *looks worried, uncomfortable, trapped under* BRUNO'S *incessant barrage of talk. They both smoke.*

BRUNO : Men ageing become more and more beautiful, not women. Besides I find it extraordinarily unjust for a woman to age. And I've noticed a strange thing — women, when they commit suicide, always throw themselves under a train or out of a window. They are so frightened of not going through with it that they throw themselves forward. That way, it's impossible to pull back. Men never. It's very rare for a man to throw himself on the underground line, and it's very rare for a woman to open her veins. I find that very brave, and at the same time very cowardly of them. Yes, I don't know. Life gives women a purpose, death gives men one. It is death that is important.

Close up : VERONICA.

BRUNO *off :* ' One day,' Van Gogh said, ' we will catch death to go to another star.'

BRUNO *continues to pace about.*

BRUNO : There is something more important than having an ideal, but what?

BRUNO *throws away his cigarette-end, violently.*

BRUNO : It is something more important than not being defeated. I would just love to know exactly what it is. ' Pathetic ', once, when I was at school, it was a word I admired. Now I despise it. ' Taciturn ', there's a word that is very beautiful — like William. Me, I'm lost unless I pretend to be lost. My argument is that everyone has an ideal, therefore there is something more important that everyone hasn't got. For example, I am sure that God doesn't have an ideal. There is a very, very beautiful saying. Whose is it? I think it was Lenin. ' Ethics are the aesthetics of the future.' I find that saying very beautiful and very moving as well. It reconciles the right and the left. What are they thinking of, the

78

people of the right and left? Today, revolution, why bother? Once a reactionary government gets to power, it applies left-wing policies and vice-versa. Me, I win or lose, but I fight alone. Around 1930 young people had a revolution. For example, Malraux, Drieu la Rochelle, Aragon. We no longer have anything. They had the Spanish Civil War, we haven't even got our own war. Apart from ourselves, our own face and our own voice, we have nothing. But perhaps that is what is important, to come to recognise the sound of one's own voice . . .

BRUNO *stares at himself in the mirror.*

BRUNO : . . . and the shape of one's own face. From inside, it is like this . . .

BRUNO, *his back to the camera, makes a wall around his face with the palms of his hands. Then he turns and looks straight at the camera. He remakes the wall. Now we see his knuckles blotting out his face.*

BRUNO : . . . and when I look at it, it's like that . . .

He pulls his hands away and stares fixedly, open-eyed, into the camera.

BRUNO : That is to say you look at me and you don't know what I'm thinking . . . and you will never know what I'm thinking.

As he talks he looks from side to side.

BRUNO : There, now . . . a forest in Germany, a bicycle ride . . . it is finished. Now . . . the terrace of a Barcelona café. Now . . . it is already finished.

He stares again at the camera.

BRUNO : I try to trap my own thoughts, and speech. Where does speech come from? Perhaps people talk without stopping, like gold prospectors . . .

He looks down.

BRUNO : . . . to find the truth. Instead of panning the bottom of the river, they pan the bottom of their own thoughts. They eliminate all the words that have no value and they end up

79

finding one, all alone . . . but, a single word alone . . .
He stares again at the camera.
BRUNO : . . . it's already silence.
The piano music breaks in again. BRUNO looks across at
VERONICA.
BRUNO : Why do you love me?
Close up : VERONICA looks up at him, then down,
hesitantly.
VERONICA : I don't know . . .
She smiles shyly and presses her open palm to her face.
VERONICA : . . . because I'm crazy.
BRUNO *strokes her face and picks up the telephone.*
VERONICA : Who are you ringing?
A SECRETARY *at the French News Agency picks up the*
phone.
SECRETARY : Hello, French News Agency.
In the background a news bulletin comes faintly over the
radio.

RADIO MESSAGE *over : that is why the* ■ ■ *will no longer be*
satisfied with promises or speeches and as a result demand
solemn pledges and acts ■ ■ *finally the other information that*
must be given, although with reservation; the league ■ ■ *had*
decided to give two millions in aid to ■ ■ *. . . finally as from*
tomorrow Thursday the 22nd May at 4 pm the sending of
telegrams between Metropolitan France and Algeria is once
again allowed, as long as the telegrams are clearly made out in
French.

JACQUES, *telephone in hand.*
JACQUES : Yes, put him through.
He signals to PAUL, who starts a miniature tape recorder.
JACQUES : Hello, who's that? Who's that?
JACQUES *and* PAUL *record* BRUNO'S *replies.*

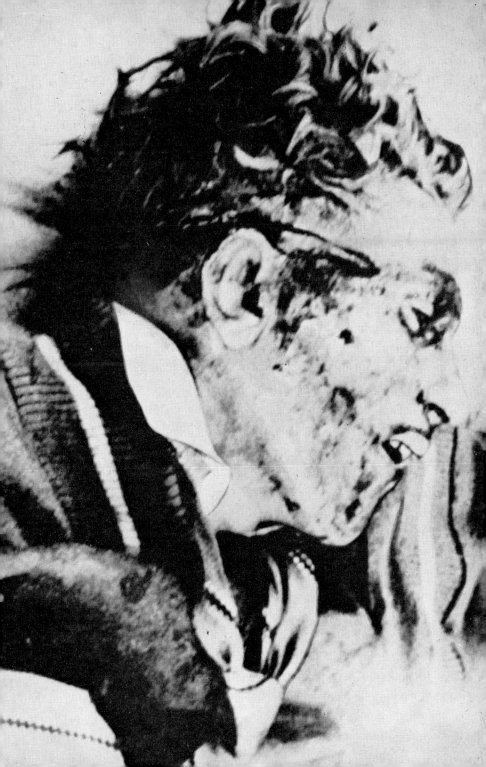

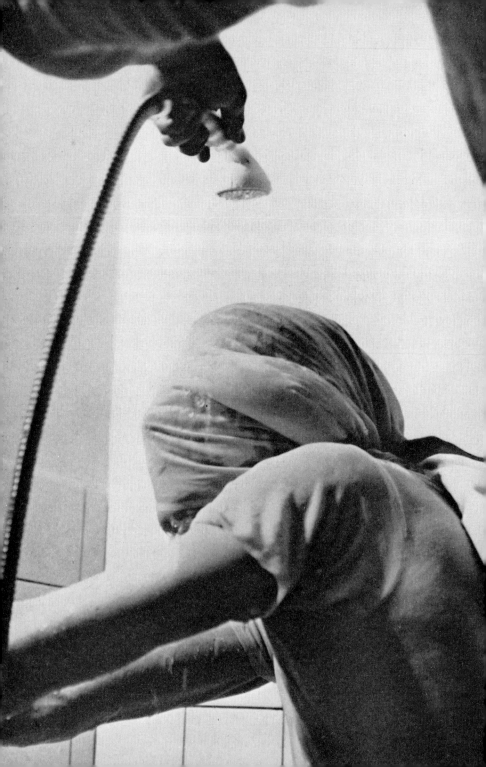

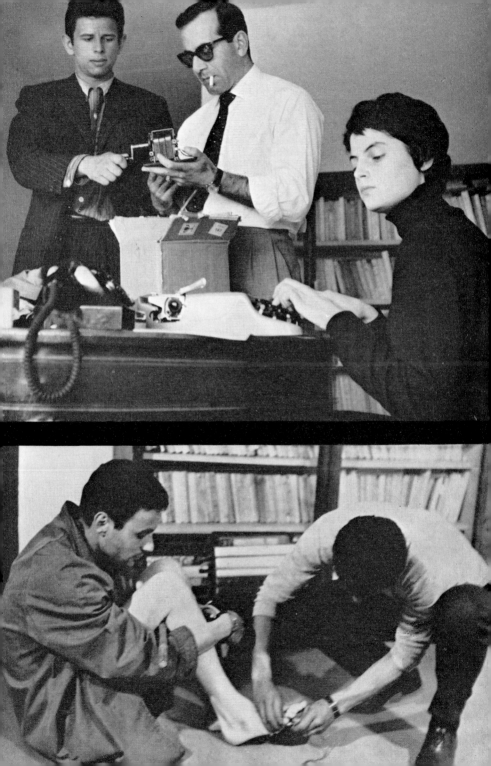

BRUNO: It's Bruno.

Close up : BRUNO at the telephone.

VERONICA: What's the matter?

BRUNO: Bruno Forestier . . . What do you mean, it's fake. Perhaps they've moved, they must be suspicious.

JACQUES at the telephone.

JACQUES: I've just been there with Paul. No Mohammed Messoussa at that address.

JACQUES looks across at PAUL who nods and turns off the tape recorder.

BRUNO *off :* Conclusion: no passports for me and Veronica unless, of course, I decide to kill Arthur Palivoda.

JACQUES *into the telephone :* Okay, come on over here.

The piano music breaks in again.

JACQUES and PAUL play back the tape recording : 'BRUNO, BRUNO FORESTIER.'

PAUL: You're a genius!

JACQUES: Thanks, you're too kind.

JACQUES *into the telephone :* Okay, see you next week.

JACQUES looks at VERONICA'S photo on his desk.

JACQUES: You were right, Paul, a girl, alone in life, she is either a whore or an informer. The F.L.N. — they must have another address, and she must know it.

JACQUES hands a revolver to PAUL, who picks it up together with the tape recorder. They leave the office and get into the Peugeot.

BRUNO paces around the room in VERONICA'S apartment.

BRUNO: Lock yourself in, you never know with them.

VERONICA stands against the wall.

VERONICA: They knew you've been tortured?

BRUNO stands leaning against the room-divider and stares at VERONICA. He rubs his face.

BRUNO: Yes. I'm happy. The police found my Chevrolet on the Swiss road.

VERONICA: When will you be back?

BRUNO : I must flush out Palivoda. Maybe this evening . . .
or tomorrow. It's pretty, that dress.

The camera pans to VERONICA.

VERONICA : Yes, it's a present.

BRUNO : Is it from the guy who was giving you a little dog
the first time we met? Did you sleep with him?

BRUNO *comes up behind* VERONICA *and spins her round
to face him. She turns away and* BRUNO *walks off.*

VERONICA : He has been chasing me for ages.

She turns to face BRUNO.

VERONICA : It's not important.

The camera pans to BRUNO.

BRUNO : Yes. Oh yes, but it is.

BRUNO *gives his clenched fist salute.*

BRUNO : Hasta luego.

VERONICA *salutes.*

VERONICA : Be seeing you.

*The camera pans down the face of the building. Piano
music breaks in. The Peugeot draws up ouside*
VERONICA'S *apartment block.* JACQUES *and* PAUL *jump
out and rush to hide behind the emergency staircase as*
BRUNO *comes out.* BRUNO *looks up once towards*
VERONICA'S *apartment and runs off.* JACQUES *and* PAUL
*dodge inside and the camera pans back up the face of
the building.* JACQUES *and* PAUL *get out of the lift.* PAUL
is carrying the miniature tape recorder. JACQUES *rings
the bell to* VERONICA'S *apartment.* PAUL *holds the open
recorder up to the door. When* VERONICA *calls through
the door,* BRUNO'S *voice answers from the recorder.*

VERONICA : Who is that?

RECORDED VOICE OF BRUNO : It's Bruno.

VERONICA : Who is there? Is that you, Bruno?

RECORDED VOICE OF BRUNO : It's Bruno, Bruno Forestier.
Forestier.

VERONICA *opens the door.* JACQUES *and* PAUL *grab her,*

86

*take away her gun and, covering her, push her up against
the wall.*

BRUNO *rushes through streets crowded with pedestrians
and traffic.*

BRUNO *off :* Then, everything happened very quickly and the
situation, which seemed very complex, worked itself out very
simply. While I went to the meeting they had fixed with
me . . .

Close up : VERONICA'S *handcuffed wrists. The camera
pans up to her face. She is being driven away by*
JACQUES *and* PAUL *in the Peugeot. The wind blows her
sunlit hair. She looks beautiful and vulnerable.*

BRUNO *off :* . . . The French shut Veronica up in a lakeside
villa. There they tortured her horribly . . .

*From a distance the camera watches the Peugeot pull
off the road and the door open.*

BRUNO *off :* . . . to make her give them the new address of
Palivoda's friends.

BRUNO *sits in the office of the French News Agency,
waiting.*

BRUNO *off :* But I didn't know that yet.

JACQUES *comes in reading an evening paper.*

BRUNO : Jacques only told me he was holding Veronica
hostage.

*In a continuation of the same distant shot of the Peugeot,
we see* VERONICA *trying to run away, and being grabbed
by* PAUL.

BRUNO *off :* She would be returned to me, he said, once I
had killed Palivoda. At the same time as the passports.

Piano music.

BRUNO *and* JACQUES *walk up to a parked car.*

BRUNO *sticks a gun in his belt.*

JACQUES : You must have the strength sometimes to cut your
way with a dagger.

Close up : The gun in Bruno's *fist as he walks along a street.*

Close up : Palivoda *walking with a girl.*

From across the street the camera follows as Bruno *walks just behind* Palivoda, *his gun pointing at* Palivoda's *back. Suddenly* Bruno *fires,* Palivoda *falls.* Bruno *rushes across the street towards the camera.*

Bruno *off :* It was after killing Palivoda that I learnt of Veronica's death.

Police siren.

Bruno, *still holding the gun, comes up an escalator.*

Bruno *off :* Only one thing was left to me : learn not to be bitter. But I was happy, because I had a lot of time in front of me.

Bruno *puts away his gun, buttons his jacket and hurries out into a quiet, sunlit, listless street.*

FILMOGRAPHY

Features

1959   A Bout de Souffle (Breathless)

Script by Jean-Luc Godard. Based on an idea by François Truffaut. Directed by Jean-Luc Godard. Photography by Raoul Coutard.
Cast : Jean-Paul Belmondo, Jean Seberg.

1960   Le Petit Soldat (The Little Soldier)

Script and direction by Jean-Luc Godard. Photography by Raoul Coutard.
Cast : Michel Subor, Anna Karina.
(Refused distribution by French Censor Board and the Minister of Information until January 1963.)

1961   Une Femme est une Femme (A Woman is a Woman)

Script by Jean-Luc Godard. Based on an idea by Geneviève Cluny. Directed by Jean-Luc Godard. Photography (Techniscope and Eastman Colour) by Raoul Coutard.
Cast : Anna Karina, Jean-Paul Belmondo, Jean-Claude Brialy.

1962   Vivre sa Vie (My Life to Live)

Script and direction by Jean-Luc Godard. Photography Raoul Coutard.
Cast : Anna Karina, Sady Rebbot, André S. Labarthe.

1963   Les Carabiniers (The Soldiers)

Script by Jean-Luc Godard, Jean Gruault, Roberto Rossellini. Based on the play *I Carabinieri* by Benjamino Joppolo. Directed by Jean-Luc Godard. Photography by Raoul Coutard.
Cast : Marino Masè, Albert Juross, Geneviève Galéa, Catherine Ribéro.

89

1963   Le Mépris (Contempt)

Script by Jean-Luc Godard. Based on the novel *Il Disprezzo* by Alberto Moravia. Directed by Jean-Luc Godard. Photography (Franscope and Technicolor) by Raoul Coutard.
Cast : Brigitte Bardot, Michel Piccoli, Jack Palance.

1964   Bande à Part (Band of Outsiders)

Script by Jean-Luc Godard. Based on the novel *Fool's Gold* by Dolores Hitchens. Directed by Jean-Luc Godard. Photography by Raoul Coutard.
Cast : Anna Karina, Claude Brasseur, Sami Frey.

1964   Une Femme Mariée (The Married Woman)

Script and direction by Jean-Luc Godard. Photography by Raoul Coutard.
Cast : Macha Méril, Bernard Noël, Philippe Leroy.

1965   Alphaville, ou Une Etrange Aventure de Lemmy Caution.

Script and direction by Jean-Luc Godard. Photography by Raoul Coutard.
Cast : Eddie Constantine, Anna Karina, Howard Vernon, Akim Tamiroff.

1965   Pierrot Le Fou

Script by Jean-Luc Godard. Based on the novel *Obsession* by Lionel White. Directed by Jean-Luc Godard. Photography (Techniscope and Eastman Colour) by Raoul Coutard.
Cast : Jean-Paul Belmondo, Anna Karina.

1966   Masculin-Féminin

Script by Jean-Luc Godard. Based on *La Femme de Paul* and *Le Signe* by Guy de Maupassant. Directed by Jean-Luc Godard. Photography by Willy Kurant.
Cast : Jean-Pierre Léaud, Chantal Goya, Catherine-Isabelle Duport.

1966   Made In USA

Script by Jean-Luc Godard. Based on the novel *Rien dans le coffre* by Richard Stark. Directed by Jean-Luc Godard. Photography (Techniscope and Eastman Colour) by Raoul Coutard.
Cast : Anna Karina, Laszlo Szabo, Jean-Pierre Léaud.

1966   Deux ou Trois Choses que je sais d'elle

Script and direction by Jean-Luc Godard. Photography (Techniscope and Eastman Colour) by Raoul Coutard.
Cast : Marina Vlady, Anny Duperey, Roger Montsoret.

1967   La Chinoise, ou plutôt à la Chinoise

Script and direction by Jean-Luc Godard. Photography (Eastman Colour) by Raoul Coutard.
Cast: Anne Wiazemsky, Jean-Pierre Léaud, Michel Sémeniako.

1967   Loin du Viêt-nam (Far from Vietnam)

Directors : Alain Resnais, William Klein, Joris Ivens, Claude Lelouch, Jean-Luc Godard. Agnès Varda's episode was not included. Eastman Colour.

1967   Weekend

Script and direction by Jean-Luc Godard. Photography (Eastman Colour) by Raoul Coutard.
Cast : Mireille Darc, Jean Yanne.

1968   Le Gai Savoir

Script and direction by Jean-Luc Godard. Photography (Eastman Colour) by Jean Leclerc.
Cast : Juliet Berto, Jean-Pierre Léaud.

1968   Un Film Comme Les Autres

No information is available on this film. It had a public screening early in 1969 at the Philharmonic Hall in New York.

1968   One Plus One

Script and direction by Jean-Luc Godard. Photography (Eastman Colour) by Tony Richmond.

Cast : The Rolling Stones, Anne Wiazemsky, Ian Quarrier.

1968/69   One American Movie/1 A.M.

Script and direction by Jean-Luc Godard. Photography by D. A. Pennebaker and Richard Leacock.

Cast: Eldridge Cleaver, Tom Hayden, LeRoi Jones, Rip Torn, The Jefferson Airplane.

1969   British Sounds

Script and direction by Jean-Luc Godard. Photography (Eastman Colour) by Charles Stewart.

1969   Le Vent d'Est

Script by Daniel Cohn-Bendit. Directed by Jean-Luc Godard. Photography (Eastman Colour) by Mario Vulpiano.

Cast : Gian Maria Volonté, Anne Wiazemsky, Daniel Cohn-Bendit.

Shorts

1954 — Opération Béton.

1955 — Une Femme Coquette.

1957 — Tous les Garçons s'appellent Patrick.

1958 — Charlotte et son Jules.

1958 — Une Histoire d'Eau (with Truffaut).

Sketches

1961 — La Paresse (sketch in *Les Sept Péchés Capitaux*)

1962 — Le Nouveau Monde (sketch in *RoGoPaG*)

1963 — Le Grand Escroc (sketch in *Les Plus Belles Escroqueries du Monde*)

1963 — Montparnasse-Levallois (sketch in *Paris vu par . . .*)

1967 — Anticipation, ou L'An 2,000 (sketch in *Le Plus Vieux Métier du Monde ou L'Amour à travers les Ages*)

1967 — L'Enfant Prodigue (sketch in *Vangelo '70*)

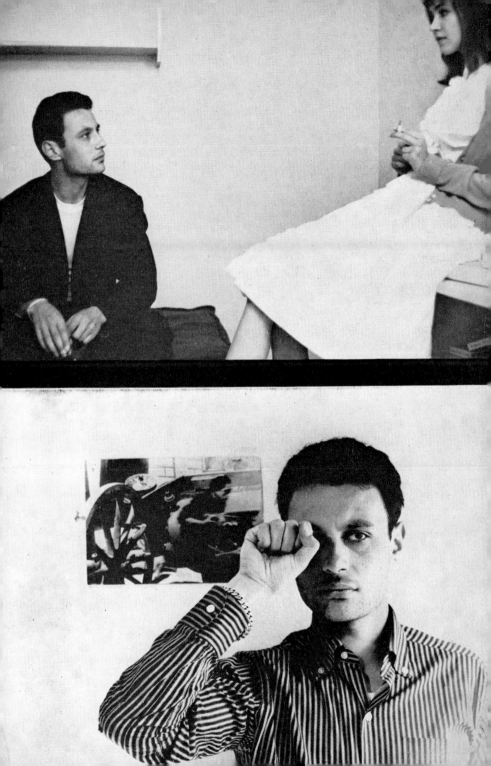